Communities of
Resistance and Solidarity

Communities of Resistance and Solidarity

A Feminist Theology of Liberation

Sharon D. Welch

ORBIS BOOKS

Maryknoll, New York 10545

Second Printing, December 1985

The Catholic Foreign Mission Society of America (Maryknoll) recruits and trains people for overseas missionary service. Through Orbis Books Maryknoll aims to foster the international dialogue that is essential to mission. The books published, however, reflect the opinions of their authors and are not meant to represent the official position of the society.

Library of Congress Cataloging in Publication Data

Welch, Sharon D.
  Communities of resistance and solidarity.

  Bibliography: p.
  Includes index.
  1. Woman (Theology)   2. Liberation theology.
3. Revolutions—Religious aspects.   I. Title.
BL458.W45   1985   230   85-4809
ISBN 0-88344-204-3 (pbk.)

To my parents,
James Welch
and
Reta Graef Welch

Contents

Preface

What does it mean to be a Christian theologian in the late twentieth century? What does it mean to be, more precisely, a feminist, white, middle-class, American Christian theologian? What does it mean to act as a person of faith, to reflect on one's faith, within these parameters?

These questions have not always been the ones that marked the beginning of theological discourse. They do, however, mark the beginning of theological discourse for me and for many others. These questions are not derived from the enterprise of theology in itself, but emerge from an experience of faith that is increasingly predominant in our time, an experience of faith in which one becomes aware of one's role in society as oppressor or as victim of oppression.

The proliferation of theologies of liberation—feminist, black, Latin American, Asian—all reflect this particular experience of faith. My work also reflects this dynamic. My participation in a community of faith has evoked an awareness of my oppression as a woman, and has enabled and compelled my resistance to that oppression. I feel a real kinship with other liberation theologians, and see, therefore, my work as being the development of a feminist theology of liberation.

There is another aspect, however, to my experience of faith, one identified by the terms *white, middle-class*, and *American*. For me, to be a Christian is to become aware of the degree to which I am a participant in structures of oppression, structures of race, class, and national identity. As a woman, I am oppressed by the structures of patriarchy. Yet as white, I benefit from the oppression of people of other races. As a person whose economic level is middle-class, I am both victim and victimizer of others. As an American, I live within a nation whose policies are economically, politically, and environmentally disastrous for far too many of the world's peoples.

This book is an attempt to respond theologically to my double identity—oppressor and oppressed. My turning to the categories of faith and the intellectual enterprise of theology is not arbitrary, but is grounded in the actual matrix of my awareness of both of these phenomena, that matrix being my participation in Christian communities of faith. These communities of faith have been both traditional and nontraditional—the church of my childhood, the congregations I have attended as an adult, and communities of faithful political resistance. This work would not have been possible without my participation in the women's community at Vanderbilt Divinity School, the

Nashville chapter of Clergy and Laity Concerned, the Memphis Nuclear Weapons Freeze Campaign, the women's community at Harvard Divinity School, and the peace community at Harvard Divinity School.

My work has been guided by friends who are activists, by friends who are theologians, and by friends who are fully committed to both enterprises. I am especially indebted to the faculty at Vanderbilt who guided this work in its earlier formulation as a dissertation: Edward Farley, Peter Hodgson, Eugene TeSelle, Sallie McFague. Many good friends gave me encouragement and criticism: Pack Matthews, Mary Fulkerson, Mark Sullivan, Betty DeBerg, Paul Lakeland, Russell Gregory, Marilyn Massey, Sharon Parks, and Gordon Kaufman. These people challenged me to pursue both intellectual rigor and personal and political honesty.

Although I examine a single theme—a political interpretation of the truth of Christian faith—my argument is far from linear. Central themes are returned to again and again; no single conclusion or set of definitive theses is presented. I have, rather, outlined a perspective, a guiding set of questions and concerns. The questioning nature of this work is not accidental but is directly correlated with my own political and personal situation. I shall not pretend to have reached in theory a maturity I have yet to achieve in life. I am, quite frankly, a novice—a novice feminist, a novice political activist, a novice theologian.

1

The Fundamental Crisis in Christian Theology

It is at least audacious if not anachronistic to be a theologian in this present era, the era of the end of Christendom. Liberal theology is undergoing a fundamental crisis. Its problems are not merely superficial or internal, but concern the nature of theology as a particular form of discourse and as a discourse in relation to other discourses. Internally, the problem is partially one of the type of language appropriate to theology, whether to employ narrative, ontological discourse, or metaphorical language, to speak of faith and its apprehensions of world, self, and deity. Liberal theologians also face the problem of discerning the types of truth-claims appropriate to the object of theology, the divine-human relationship.[1]

If these were the only difficulties facing liberal theologians, the problem could be rather easily solved. The problem is, however, much deeper. As Edward Farley states in *Ecclesial Man*, the crisis of theology is found in the problem beneath the problem of theological method. This prior problem concerns the reality referent of Christian faith and thus of Christian theology. Liberal theologians must not only examine the adequacy of their language about God; they must also question the very reality of God. Theological questioning moves also at this fundamental level, attempting to establish that the word *God* is not only *appropriate* as a signifier, but actually signifies something. As Farley clearly states, if Christian faith has no referent, the problem of theological method is a meaningless one. The prior problem for any liberal theologian, the problem that must be addressed before one delves into the problem of method, is the identification of the locus of faith's reality, the delineation of the reality referent of this particular form of discourse (Farley 1975, 8–9).

There are several ways of addressing this problem facing liberal theologians. In one sense it is a perennial issue, a dilemma caused by the uniqueness of the referent of theology and the attempt of people of faith to speak in human terms, to know through the human mind, that which transcends the

1

human. This way of posing the problem is as old as theology itself. It is reflected in Paul's "seeing through a glass darkly" (1 Cor. 13:12), in Aquinas's assessment of his *Summa* as straw, in Luther's appeal to the God beyond God (Luther 1959, 57), in Tillich's reminder that serious doubt is a necessary concomitant of ultimate concern (Tillich 1957, 16–22).

THE CONCEPTUAL INADEQUACY OF CHRISTIAN THEOLOGY

An initial consideration of these earlier expressions of doubt and inadequacy may be comforting. Liberal theologians are not the first people to struggle with the adequacy of their language about faith and about God. Yet this solace evaporates as we consider the basic assumption behind these earlier demurrals of certainty. Paul, Aquinas, Luther, and Tillich all assume that faith refers to something real, an experience of ultimacy that is in some way actual and present, an ultimacy that limits and shapes the nature of theological inquiry (Tillich 1973, 131). We modern academic theologians no longer have the surety of such a referent. The "masters of suspicion," Nietzsche, Marx, and Freud (Ricoeur 1974, 148), have effaced this refuge for theologians, this assurance that their language refers to a dimension of ultimacy (Ricoeur 1974, 442).

Ricoeur analyzed the impact of the atheistic critique of religion (on intellectuals, I must add, although Ricoeur does not so delimit his work), its critique of the intellectual honesty and moral propriety of theology and Christian faith (Ricoeur 1974, 440–459). Freud concluded that our sense of the transcendent was illusory; Nietzsche claimed that it was an expression of *"ressentiment,"* the vituperation of the weak against the strong; Marx argued that it was a poignant but ineffectual protest against suffering. I would add to these "masters of suspicion" the radical feminist Mary Daly, who finds in Christian faith and theology not a reference to God or the ultimate but a denial of life. Her statement that "patriarchy is the prevailing religion of the entire planet and its essential message is necrophilia" is an assessment of the Christian faith's perception of the transcendent as an illusory and deadly escape from a world of becoming and finitude (Daly 1978, 39).

A radical critique of theology and of Christian faith, a critique both of the adequacy of theological method and the reality of faith's referent, is not new. This problem begins to emerge quite clearly in the nineteenth century in debates about theological method. Theologians were seeking intellectually respectable standards of evidence, credible ways of making claims for the truth of Christian faith in light of developments in the natural and historical sciences (Welch 1972, 5). The disclosure of the "ugly ditch of history" (Lessing) led to formulations of the nature of Christian faith and its correlative theological method that were not dependent on historically accurate portrayals of the life of Jesus (Welch 1972, 314).

This approach continued into the twentieth century in neo-orthodox theology in the work of Barth and Bultmann, Gogarten, and others (Zahrnt

1966, chaps. 1–4). Theologians tried to respond to Hume's and Kant's philosophical critiques of theology and its claims by locating the matrix of theological insight in aspects of human experience other than the intellect, and by developing a mode of reflection that accepted that limitation: Coleridge and his location of faith in the imagination, Schleiermacher and his Kantian approach to theology, limiting it to the expression of the religious affections set forth in speech (Coleridge 1883; Schleiermacher 1928, 76). Many liberal theologians continue to emphasize the nonrational or prerational aspects of faith and thus argue that its expression should not compete with that of philosophy, for it represents another area of human inquiry and understanding. Paul Ricoeur and Sallie McFague, for example, claim that the language of faith is metaphorical and poetic, not metaphysical or anthropological (Ricoeur 1975; McFague 1975).

As imaginative and helpful as these approaches to the problem of theological method have been, they have failed to lay to rest the ghost of Feuerbach. Despite the protestations of his triviality by Barth, Feuerbach continues to haunt us and has even been joined by many others. Theologians may not be convinced by Feuerbach's critique of religion as projection, but neither can they readily refute it. Liberal theologians have not yet discovered the type of evidence and style of argument that can establish with sufficient certainty the reality of God, nor have they definitively outlined the theological method that is appropriate for this region of reality.

THE MORAL INADEQUACY OF CHRISTIAN FAITH

The theological problems of demonstrating the reality of God and of clarifying the proper style of theological argument and language are stimulating and challenging for theologians, but they are not the problems that most concern people of faith. The second area of concern that I wish to address is a moral one, and, as such, is shared by theologians and by people of faith. While I find the methodological problems facing theology intellectually challenging, the moral problems are deeply threatening.

Is Christian faith itself ideological? Is it a dangerous mask for relations of domination? Feminist theologians are beginning to ask questions like these of Christianity, pointing to the complicity of the Christian tradition in the oppression of women. Compared to Mary Daly's critique of Christian faith and theology, the challenge of Feuerbach seems genteel and innocuous. Her challenge is not just to the conceptual inadequacy of Christian theology. She questions the moral adequacy of Christian faith and theology. It is not just the expression or the use of Christian symbols that she charges with ideology; she denounces the very substance of that faith and its theology as ideological. Mary Daly claims that Christian faith itself is an expression of patriarchy and necrophilia (Daly 1978, 39).

The challenge of Mary Daly raises serious questions, questions that are exacerbated by other radical critiques of Christian faith and theology. Marxist critiques of religion, for example, also identify Christian faith with the legitimation of oppression (Marx 1964, 41–42; Míguez 1976, 49–50). These critiques, the feminist and the Marxist, shatter the complacency of faith. They remind us that the history of Christianity and its impact on society is checkered at best. The atrocities of the Inquisition, the witchburnings, the Crusades, the justification of imperialism and colonialism, the perpetuation of sexism, racism, anti-Semitism, the silence of most churches in the face of the horrors of war and the Nazi holocaust should cause even the most committed Christian to question the truth of Christianity's claims (Johnson 1979).

Does Christian faith actually have as a referent, given the atrocity of Christian complicity with injustice and hatred throughout the centuries, a God who is both loving and just? The truth of Christian faith and theology—the existence or reality of its referent—is called into question not only by intellectual quandaries but also by the actual practice of that faith in history.

THE THEOLOGICAL AND POLITICAL CHALLENGE OF LIBERATION FAITH

These challenges to Christian faith are serious, yet they do not necessarily constitute a final refutation of its moral adequacy. There are movements within Christianity that criticize it harshly, but develop their criticism from within the locus of faith. Liberation theology is a response to the moral challenge to Christianity. The "underground church," the base Christian communities, the involvement of Christians in liberation struggles—all are expressions of a Christian faith that criticizes those aspects of the Christian tradition that are oppressive in the name of a particular God, a God of justice.

I find in liberation theology as it now exists the possibility of a way out of the crisis that confronts liberal theology. Yet in my attempt to reflect on Christian faith in the matrix of a struggle against oppression, I am still confronted by fundamental intellectual and moral problems. These problems are superficially similar to those faced by liberal theologians. The problem of the reality of faith's referent remains unresolved. Yet there are significant differences in the nature of the theological task when the grounds for questioning the existence of God are moral rather than intellectual.

The criterion of liberation faith and liberation theology is practice, or, more specifically, the process of liberation in history. Here is a specific interpretation of the scriptural dictum that "the truth will make you free" (Jn. 8:32). But how does "truth" free? Where is the liberating God found in history? What does it mean to take the Nicaraguan revolution as evidence of the reality of the liberating God in light of the continued threats to that new government by the United States and in light of the thwarted revolutions in Chile and El Salvador? Where was a liberating God in the Nazi holocaust, or in the lemming-like rush to nuclear holocaust by the United States and the Soviet Union?

The power and ambiguity of this form of liberation faith is that just as it succeeds in producing awareness of a liberating God who evokes solidarity with other people, an affirmation of the significance of human life and thus protest against suffering and oppression, the reality of that God is called into question by the "dangerous memory" of the dead, of all those who have suffered without apparent liberation.[2] To avoid a too facile faith in the power of liberation, we theologians of liberation must ask about the meaning of the cross and resurrection, about the reality of a redeeming, liberating God in light of the barbarities of the twentieth century: the holocaust, Vietnam, Hiroshima-Nagasaki, sexism, racism, the nuclear arms race, the torture of political prisoners.

Children of Violence

My attempt to develop a feminist theology of liberation is motivated by my experience of the total breakdown of given modes of order and classification when I confront the twentieth century's banal yet deadly entrapment in mass murder and exploitation. It is all too easy to evade the weight of the inhumanity of the twentieth century. The means of evasion are many: a focus on scientific progress; a "mature" recognition of the persistence of human evil; a naive adherence to the ideal of the ultimate triumph of non-violence and justice. Doris Lessing challenges this evasion by reminding us of the shocking disparity between humane ideals and the tragedy of human life. In this passage from her book *Landlocked,* Thomas rejects Martha's pleas to forego armed resistance and return to his former adherence to pacifism.

> She said to him, "Thomas, if you do this, you'll put yourself outside everything you believe."
> "Are you telling me what I believe, Martha? What difference does it make what I believe. In the last decade forty million human beings were murdered and so many millions crippled, wounded, starved, stunted and driven mad that we'll never count them. . . . Two years ago the British and the Americans dropped an atom bomb on the Japanese out of military curiosity. . . . At this moment millions of people are involved in a civil war in China, but Martha does not believe in violence."
> Martha did not believe in violence. Martha was the essence of violence, she had been conceived, bred, fed and reared on violence. . . . The soul of the human race, that part of the mind which has no name, is not called Thomas and Martha, which holds the human race as frogspawn is held in jelly—that part of Martha and of Thomas was twisted and warped, was part of a twist and a damage—she could no more disassociate herself from the violence done her than a tadpole can live out of water. Forty-odd million human beings had been murdered, deliberately or from carelessness, from lack of imagination; these people had

been killed yesterday, in the last dozen years, they were dying now, as she stood under the tree, and these deaths were marked on her soul [Lessing 1964, 462–463].

My work in theology is born out of this unthinkable horror, out of the shattering of concepts of sin and redemption, concepts of a merciful and loving God, caused by the twentieth century's stark brutality—a brutality that kills millions and is carried out through the active and passive complicity of good Christians and solid citizens. If the Christians of Germany could not stop Hitler, and if the Christians of the United States cannot stop what may be the ultimate holocaust—nuclear war—of what value is Christianity? What does it mean to believe in a God of justice in the face of unthinkable injustice? What does it mean to believe in nonviolence and in liberation when we are all "children of violence"?

Moral concerns of this magnitude have led me and others to question the fundamental morality of Christian faith and Christian theology. Gordon Kaufman, for example, in his discussion of the tasks of theology in light of the threat of nuclear war, asks if we can use any of our symbols and doctrines to respond to the threat of total genocide. He especially questions the value of such concepts as the sovereignty of God, and in so doing makes a radical move for a theologian, arguing that a central symbol of the tradition is not merely inadequate but is positively dangerous, blinding us to the deadly exercise of human freedom in building and using nuclear weapons (Kaufman 1983, 3–14).

What is the rationality of a faith that blinds while using the language of final revelation? What is the meaning of doctrines and symbols that claim to reveal ultimate truth about human life but are in that life the correlates of structures of oppression, exploitation, and terror? What does it mean to believe in a gospel of love, justice, and peace when a Christian head of state, General Rios Montt, was systematically and brutally exterminating the Indian population of his country, Guatemala?

Violence and the God of Liberation

As a feminist theologian of liberation I cannot evade the ambiguity of the idea of a God who liberates. What is the referent of this language of a liberating God, a language that is central to base Christian communities, to the black church, and to the theologies that have emerged from the matrix of political resistance?

The traditional way of addressing the meaning of such language is one that I choose to reject. The traditional approach would lead me to the type of work found in fundamental theology, the attempt to correlate language about God with ontological structures and the attempt to develop a coherent and consistent pattern of referring to the divine and to things ultimate. An example of this approach is the work of process theologians, an articulation of the nature of God's action in history utilizing the White-headian categories of the primordial and consequent natures of God to provide a foundation for a discussion of any particular activity of God, such as liberation.[3] Using this approach, the phrase "liberating God" would refer to either an ontological structure or, to use Tillichian language, to that which grounds ontology. In any case, the referent of the term is somehow active in history yet is, nonetheless, a reality that is not exhausted by the historical event of liberation.

The meaning of the phrase "liberating God" is not so clear-cut in theologies of liberation. It is possible to interpret liberation theologies as consonant with the Western theological tradition; many liberation theologians themselves choose this type of interpretation (Sobrino 1980). There is, however, another way of interpreting this language—emphasizing that the referent of the phrase "liberating God" is not primarily *God* but *liberation*. That is, the language here is true not because it corresponds with something in the divine nature but because it leads to actual liberation in history. The truth of God-language and of all theological claims is measured not by their correspondence to something eternal but by the fulfillment of its claims in history, by the actual creation of communities of peace, justice, and equality.

The ambiguity of this different concept of the truth-referent of God-language can be seen in the work of liberation theologians. Sobrino, for example, offered a complex discussion of God and liberation in his presentation at the Theology in the Americas Conference in 1980. Sobrino, a Salvadoran theologian, was asked if the people of El Salvador, who are being so brutally persecuted, ever question the existence of God. He claimed that such a question was not an important one to the Christians who were being persecuted; they knew that God was with them in their suffering. The question about God that was of relevance to the Salvadorans was the question of the struggle of this God of liberation with other gods, the gods of capitalism and the national security state. Sobrino stated that in El Salvador capitalism and the national security state function as gods; they function as absolutes, as the premise of analysis and social structures, and are not subject to evaluation themselves. He also identified capitalism and the national security state as idols and as false gods because of their demands—they both require victims. The capitalist economy of El Salvador has caused the death of many people through chronic malnutrition, persistent unemployment, and poverty. Eighty percent of Salvadoran children are malnourished; forty-five percent of the population are underemployed or unemployed (Lernoux 1982, 62). The establishment and maintenance of the national security state has caused the deaths of thousands of people since 1974 (Lernoux 1982, 61–80).

In Sobrino's discussion of God, the question of truth was a question of practice: forces were identified as "gods" in terms of their function in people's lives, not in terms of their correspondence to something about the divine nature in itself.

Spiritual Dimensions of Feminist Resistance

The ambiguity of the language of a liberating God and of the truth-claims pertinent to such language is heightened as we consider the expressions of faith found in nontheistic feminist spirituality. This language is religious despite its absence of explicit talk about God because it does refer to dimensions of ultimacy. It is important to examine this language in relation to more theistic theologies of liberation because it has the same referent: the actual, historical process of liberation and resistance.

Adrienne Rich describes this feminist spirituality as "casting one's lot" with those who resist, of continuing to affirm life in the midst of systematic denials of life. Her evocation of resistance and hope is as powerful as that of theistic liberation theologians.

> My heart is moved by all I cannot save:
> so much has been destroyed
>
> I have to cast my lot with those
> who age after age, perversely,
>
> with no extraordinary power,
> reconstitute the world [Rich 1978a, 67].

But what is the "truth" of these claims? To what do they refer? Adrienne Rich holds that in feminist expressions of hope, resistance, and community among women, a new language is being born:

> two women, eye to eye
> measuring each other's spirit, each other's
> limitless desire,
>   a whole new poetry beginning here
>   [Rich 1978b, 76].

What is this new poetry that values and celebrates paradox, independence and interrelatedness, the intricacy and ultimacy of particular lives? What is this new theology that responds to political terror and economic exploitation, that is, in Archbishop Romero's terms, the voice of the voiceless (Lernoux 1982, xvii–xviii)? In interpreting this poetry and this theology I have chosen to focus on its novelty, not on its continuity with earlier forms of thought. Two factors compel me to do this: my desire to be faithful to the radical moral challenge and new political complexion of liberation faith, and my conclusion that there are fundamental distortions in the categories of Western thought.

THE TRANSFORMATION OF THE MODERN EPISTEME

The many new developments in Christian faith and practice and in feminist spirituality offer promising and challenging sources for reflection. It is possible that they represent a resolution of the crisis of liberal theology. It is my thesis that neither the crisis nor the resolution are isolated events but occur as part of an epistemic shift that is shattering the foundations of Western knowledge and action. In the work of Michel Foucault I find an incisive, unsettling description of this shift, of the collapse of the meaning of language, and of its relation to reality.

The breakdown of theology is not accidental, but occurs in the context of a wider epistemic shift, one described by Michel Foucault in his many works, but most pointedly in *The Order of Things*. The title of this book in its English translation appears to be intentionally ironic: in this work Foucault describes the tenuous nature of humanity's determinations of order, the ever-shifting panorama of the relation between words and things.

In *The Order of Things*, Foucault discusses an example of a different ordering of things that shocked him into an appreciation of how radical differences in categories of knowing can be. He describes a passage in Borges that "shattered . . . all the familiar landmarks of my thought." The passage cites a Chinese encyclopedia in which animals are divided into "(*a*) belonging to the Emperor, (*b*) embalmed, (*c*) tame, (*d*) sucking pigs, (*e*) sirens, (*f*) fabulous, (*g*) stray dogs, (*h*) included in the present classification, (*i*) frenzied, (*j*) innumerable, (*k*) drawn with a very fine camel's hair brush, (*l*) etcetera, (*m*) having just broken the water pitcher, (*n*) that from a long way off look like flies" (Foucault 1973, xv).

Foucault finds this ordering amusing and enlightening: "In the wonderment of this taxonomy, the thing we apprehend in one great leap . . . is the limitation of our [system of thought], the stark impossibility of thinking *that*" (Foucault 1973, xv). According to Foucault, it is not possible for us to understand the rationale, the reason, that connects these divisions. Of what are they divisions? What is the unity here divided (Foucault, 1973, xvi)? This is the work of "a culture devoted to the ordering of space, but it does not distribute the multiplicity of things into the categories that make it possible for us to name, speak and think" (Foucault 1973, xix).

In his histories of the changes in discourse Foucault finds a similar strangeness, the "constant verticality of the tragic, of limits set by madness and death," not a triumphant, intelligible, horizontal march toward scientificity and truth. Far from recounting humankind's steady pursuit of truth, Foucault exposes the "history of the will to truth." He claims that there is a development, a history, of what can constitute truth, a history in which the distinction between true and false is shown to be contingent, shifting, and beyond our grasp and conscious control. He speaks, therefore, of epistemic shifts, of changes in the constitutive elements of what determines the division into true and false: Whose knowledge is given authority? What sorts of warrants are acceptable? Which institutions purvey knowledge and create knowers?

Foucault's history, or what he calls at one stage in his work "archaeology," is concerned with the episteme, the field of knowledge: what counts as knowable, who it is that knows, the impact of knowledge. Foucault examines the relations between sciences, epistemology, institutions, and political practices, and discovers "a constantly moving set of articulations, shifts, and coincidences" (Foucault 1976, 192). The apparent similarity of this concern to the sociology of knowledge is dissipated as soon as Foucault describes the positive function of what a traditional history of ideas or sociology of knowledge would identify as the factors that limit knowledge:

> The episteme is not what may be known at a given period, due account taken of inadequate techniques, mental attitudes, or the limitations imposed by tradition; it is what, in the positivity of discursive practices, makes possible the existence of epistemological figures and sciences [Foucault 1976, 192].

History of the Will to Truth

Foucault grounds the truth of an episteme in its actual existence, not in its more or less adequate correspondence to an ideal standard of knowledge. He does not attempt to justify an episteme by founding it in the "authority of an original act of giving," an act "which establishes in a transcendental subject the fact and right" of the origin of knowledge. Rather his concern is with the relation of an episteme "to the processes of historical practice" (Foucault 1976, 192).

> Truth is a thing of this world: it is produced only by virtue of multiple forms of constraint. And it induces regular effects of power. Each society has a regime of truth, its "general politics" of truth: that is, the types of discourse which it accepts and makes function as true; the mechanisms and instances which enable one to distinguish true and false statements, the means by which each is sanctioned; the techniques and procedures accorded value in the acquisition of truth; the status of those who are charged with saying what counts as true [Foucault 1980b, 131].

To follow Foucault, one must be convinced of the value of his radically historical understanding of truth. In his work, truth is removed from the realm of the absolute and is thoroughly historicized. Radical shifts from one episteme to another and radical developments within discourses such as medicine and sexuality are not due to the impetus of new discoveries but reflect changes in the practice of truth, changes in the determination of what can count as true, how truth is determined, and who determines it (Foucault 1972, 208–09).

This approach to truth is thoroughly unsettling. It shatters our sense of continuity and progress in the history of ideas. Rather than a smooth progression in which truth is gradually but assuredly approximated, Foucault finds chasms, leaps between what is even understood as true, as the object of scientific knowing of human wisdom. In his historical work Foucault discloses the creation of objects such as "man" as an object of inquiry in the eighteenth century, the creation of a disciplinary society with the rise of the human sciences, and the formation of sexuality through the discourse of the confession, and later, through the discourse of psychoanalysis.

These changes are unsettling in themselves. And yet, Foucault leads us to a consideration of another reason to be frightened by the sudden and radical changes in epistemes. He refuses to reduce epistemic change to the discovery of new objects, to a simple relation to things in themselves, or to the work of human consciousness. The episteme within which we think and act is beyond us. Its changes are not determined strictly by us, and yet, our action and thought within it participates in its transformation.

Awareness of the possibility of epistemic shifts leads Foucault to a consistent relativism. His criteria for what can count as true are similarly historical and contingent. He defends these criteria, believing them more adequate than others. He is engaged in a struggle for them and with them (in applying them, in seeing the effects of truth they produce), but he has no assurance that they will last, that other, different orders of thinking will not emerge, that his warrants and categories will not someday seem as odd as those of the fictional Chinese encyclopedia and its classification of animals as frenzied, belonging to the emperor, etc. (Foucault 1972, 208, 210–11).

The Political Economy of Truth

Throughout this work I will use the category of the episteme in describing the significance of theologies of liberation. I will argue that these theologies offer a "politics of truth" that not only differs radically from liberal academic theology but also challenges our culture's dominant episteme. In order to understand the epistemic dimensions of this challenge, it is helpful to examine briefly the politics of truth, or as Foucault calls it, the "political economy of truth" that characterizes Western technological societies.

"Truth" is centered on the form of scientific discourse and the institutions which produce it; it is subject to constant economic and political incitement (the demand for truth, as much for economic production or political power); it is the object, under diverse forms, of immense diffusion and consumption (circulating through apparatuses of education and information whose extent is relatively broad in the social body, notwithstanding certain strict limitations); it is produced and transmitted under the control, dominant if not exclusive, of a few great political and economic apparatuses (university, army, writing, media); lastly, it is the issue of a whole political debate and social confrontation ("ideological" struggles) [Foucault 1980b, 131–132].

According to Foucault, discourse is ordered in particular ways, determining what we perceive and think, and these determinations themselves are subject to radical dislocations. Foucault describes major shifts in Western thought: the move from the Renaissance apprehension of order as "the Same," as similitude, through its breakdown and the emergence of the Classical perception of order as representation, of reality as a timeless table upon which everything can be coherently and tidily displayed. The modern era and its questioning about language and history, the emergence of biology from natural history, of political economy from the analysis of wealth, of philology from general grammar—all are part of an epistemic shift. Our era also manifests a further breakdown, that of the analytic of finitude, the grounding of language and its relation to reality in terms of an analysis of human being. This break is manifest in the emergence of the countersciences—the critical inquiries of linguistics, ethnology, and psychoanalysis. These inquiries "dissolve" human being; they do not find in human being the foundation of meaning and representation, for what it means to be human is itself a particular, contingent "effect of truth," the creation of networks of power and knowledge (Foucault 1973, 312–318, 373–386).

Foucault does not accept that there is a single human way of knowing, a universal system of ordering experiences, but rather claims that there is a shifting, amorphous experience of order underneath our accepted modes of apprehending and expressing the relation of words to things and of things to each other. It is the incongruity of this transpersonal lived experience of order in relation to institutionalized systems of order that leads to the breakdown of accepted systems and the slow, painful emergence of new correlations of words and things.

The fundamental codes of a culture—those governing its language, its schemes of perception, its exchanges, its techniques, its values, the hierarchy of its practices—establish for every man [sic], from the very first, the empirical orders with which he will be at home. At the other extremity of thought, there are the scientific theories or the philosophical interpretation which explain why order exists in general, what universal law it obeys, . . . and why this particular order has been established and not some other. But between these two regions . . . lies a domain . . . which is more confused, more obscure. . . . It is here that a culture, imperceptibly deviating from the empirical orders prescribed for it by its primary codes, . . . causes them to lose their original transparency, . . . frees itself sufficiently to discover that these orders are perhaps not the only possible ones or the best ones . . . [Foucault 1973, xx].

According to Foucault the experience of order is not a static given, a secure basis for thought or action. It is rather a seething mass of contradictions, and as more definitively pointed out in his later works, it is an arena of conflict between different powers, a literal struggle not only for knowledge per se, but also a struggle that determines who will live and how, a struggle that determines who will die, and for what "grand cause." A shift in modes of ordering is not a calm transition in linguistic style. It has the character of battle: it is "bloody, lethal, and far removed from the serene ideal of the Platonic dialogue" (Foucault 1980b, 115).

In *The Order of Things* Foucault analyzes current shifts in the relation of "words and things," our inability not to question the very meaning and function of language, not to examine the reality and role of human being in the foundation of the human sciences. Foucault's archaeology of the human sciences does not merely disclose the contours of theoretical struggle in the past, an epistemic shift that offers itself to the curious intellect as an intriguing object of study and analysis. He claims that we are now experiencing a change in epistemes.

> In attempting to uncover the deepest strata of Western culture, I am restoring to our silent and apparently immobile soil its rifts, its instability, its flaws; and it is the same ground that is once more stirring under our feet [Foucault 1973, xxiv].

Epistemic Presuppositions of Liberation Theology

I will attempt to identify and explore theology's transformation within this epistemic shift. This exploration is itself the result of a particular experience of order and is part of the struggle for that order. It emerges from a particular form of ecclesia, liberation faith's re-ordering of the world of faith in light of oppression and resistance to oppression.[4]

I will make use of liberation theology in two ways. On the one hand, I am indebted to what is commonly referred to as black, feminist, Latin American, and political theology. I will attempt to delineate the epistemic shift manifest in that theology. On the other hand, my own project is a theology of liberation; it is my attempt to develop a liberating mode of theological reflection within my own situation, where I am both oppressor and oppressed. This work I refer to as a feminist theology of liberation.

Two pressing areas of concern come from my double perspective, my double identity as oppressor and oppressed: a series of intellectual questions and obstacles, and a wide range of moral dilemmas and quandaries. To think theologically today is possible only if one refuses either to evade these concerns or to submit to quiescence or despair in the face of them.

My double identity leads me to two sharply divergent attitudes toward knowledge and practice: a seemingly nihilistic relativism and a commitment to resisting oppression. The "nihilism" expresses itself as a sense that "truth" is the outcome of power struggles, as an inability to claim that Christianity is true in any significant sense outside the realm of its becoming actually true in history.

This nihilistic pole reflects my awareness of the effects of truth manifest in oppressive definitions of humanity and society. It also reflects my skepticism as a North American and my real fear that the human race might not be capable of actual conversion to the other on anything but a socially insignificant, individual scale. My nihilism, or fear of nihilism, is fueled by the deadly disparity between the ideals and the practices of Western "civilization." I contend that this nihilism must be maintained, that the events of the twentieth century make it impossible to honestly assert with any assurance the likelihood of certain knowledge and final liberation.

The second pole of this work is an affirmation of liberation, of resistance to oppression, and an attempt to understand the nature and conditions of freedom. I can still claim that theology does have a referent, not ultimacy in general, but a God who liberates. And yet this thought can remain liberating only so long as it retains its nihilistic edge. Far from being a transitory ambiguity, the tension between relativism or nihilism and universal, normative claims is constitutive of a feminist theology of liberation. This theology is the life and death struggle, both practical and conceptual, between nihilism and commitment, between despair and hope.

2

Liberation Theology and the Politics of Truth

POWER AND DISCOURSE: THE EXAMPLE OF PENOLOGY

To write theology from a matrix of faith that is intrinsically political, to realize that Christian faith at times calls the oppressor to repentance and the oppressed to liberation, requires serious attention to the relationship of the discourse of faith (its symbols, doctrines, rituals, and theological systems) to social and political structures. As a liberation theologian, I am concerned with the possibility of political and social transformation and the role that religion plays both in fostering liberation and in maintaining oppression. It is not easy for many Christians to acknowledge the oppression supported and engendered by Christian faith. The ambiguities of discourse that has both oppressive and liberating functions is indeed unsettling. Such is the case with the powerful, yet dangerous, role of Jesus as a model of sacrificial love. Mary Daly and Lark D'Helen describe the negative impact of this understanding of Jesus in the lives of women. D'Helen speaks of the solace offered by a loving savior to women who are the victims of sexual abuse and beating by their husbands. They do find comfort from this savior, but the comfort has a "catch." The love of Jesus is sacrificial; it is a love that extols the merits of innocent suffering. To emulate this model leads women to accept, rather than actively resist, their own victimization.[1]

Mary Daly sharply denounces this meaning of the sacrificial love of Jesus:

The qualities that Christianity *idealizes*, especially for women, are also those of a victim: sacrificial love, passive acceptance of suffering, humility, meekness, etc. Since these are the qualities idealized in Jesus "who died for our sins," his functioning as a model reinforces the scapegoat syndrome for women. Given the victimized situation of the female in sexist society, these "virtues" are hardly the qualities that women should be encouraged to have. Moreover, since women cannot

15

be "good" enough to measure up to this ideal, and since all are by sexual definition alien from the male savior, this is an impossible model. Thus doomed to failure even in emulating the Victim, women are plunged more deeply into victimization [Daly 1973, 77].

The meaning of the sacrificial love of Jesus is not exhausted by its internal logic or its coherence with the historically available words of Jesus, but includes the social effect of this symbol in the lives of women.

Concerns about the meaning and the political and social function of ideas and symbols are examined in Foucault's analysis of discourse. The discernment of the social and political function of symbols and images is a new task for theologians, and it requires new philosophical tools, new ways of posing questions and finding relevant evidence. Foucault's analysis of discourse clarifies the way power and discourse are related, and what is required in examining their mutual effects. Discourse is a common term, but Foucault gives it a specific meaning. He begins by referring to a traditional distinction that he no longer finds adequate, the differentiation of discursive and nondiscursive practices. Discursive practices are ideas, texts, theories, the use of language. Nondiscursive practices are social systems, class divisions, economic needs, institutions. Foucault argues that these two practices must be understood in relation to each other.

An example of their interrelation is seen in Foucault's description of the shift in medical discourse from 1770 to 1815. He describes the emergence of a new form of discourse: the clinical gaze. A change came about not only in concepts but also in the nature and social impact of institutions.

> . . . from 1770 to 1815, medical discourse changed more profoundly than since the seventeenth century, probably than since the Middle Ages, and perhaps even since Greek medicine; a change that revealed new objects, . . . techniques of observation, of detection of the pathological site, recording; a new perceptual grid, and an almost entirely new descriptive vocabulary; new sets of concepts and nosographical distributions (century-old, sometimes age-old categories such as fever or constitution disappeared, and diseases that are perhaps as old as the world—like tuberculosis—were at last isolated and named) [Foucault 1976, 170].

This description of the clinical gaze sounds suspiciously theoretical and subjective. That perception is eradicated when we realize what the gaze includes. It is not merely the mode of observation practiced by physicians. It is an apparatus that includes the shift from the family to the hospital as the primary locus of health care, the design of hospital buildings to separate and categorize diseases, the techniques of anatomy, the shift to the clinic as the primary mode of teaching medicine (Foucault 1975, 196–197).

To examine the institutional correlates of changes in discourse is to become attentive to the power of language and ideas, to their embeddedness in networks of social and political control. Foucault argues that power is productive as well as repressive, that the power of discourse is seen as much in the realities that it produces as in the forces that it binds.

What makes power hold good, what makes it accepted, is simply the fact that it doesn't only weigh on us as a force that says no, but that it traverses and produces things, it induces pleasure, forms knowledge, produces discourse. It needs to be considered as a productive network that runs through the whole social body, much more than as a negative instance whose function is repression [Foucault 1980b, 119].

In order to understand the productive aspect of discourse and its effects of truth, it is helpful to briefly consider Foucault's discussion of penology. The integration of power and knowledge in discourse is clear in Foucault's analysis of the birth of the prison, an event with ramifications far beyond penology. In the emergence of the prison, not only do we see a shift from the body to the soul as the object of punishment, but we discover strategies and techniques of power essential for the maintenance of our society, strategies that include the emergence of the human sciences. Sheridan provides an apt summation of this thesis when he states that "our own societies are maintained not by army, police, and a centralized, visible state apparatus, but precisely by those techniques of dressage, discipline, and diffused power at work in 'carceral' institutions" (Sheridan 1980, 136).

Foucault even claims that the origin of the human sciences was not merely a development in intellectual history, but came about in correlation with a new technology of power. Sheridan provides a concise statement of Foucault's thesis:

The shift away from overt punishment of the body to investigation of the criminal's "soul" can only be understood by seeing the new penal methods and the social sciences that provide the "knowledge" on which these methods are based as having a common origin. The provenance . . . of the human sciences is not a pure, disinterested search for knowledge, the fruits of which were then passed on in the "humanization" of "carceral" institutions. It is rather that those "sciences" have a common origin with those institutions [Sheridan 1980, 138].

In the *ancien régime*, the focus of punishment was the body. This was no longer the case by the 1840s. By that time public torture was no longer an accepted means of punishment. Foucault finds a shift to detention, to correction and supervision in the nineteenth century. While such moves were lauded as manifestations of a progressive, humanitarian spirit, Foucalt argues that this shift is considerably more complex. One form of coercion was replaced by another, by a technology of power that had several functions. One of these was the differentiation of crime, not the elimination or reduction of criminal behaviors. The most significant of these differentiations of crime is, ironically, regarded as the mark of the failure of penology, the creation of a delinquent subclass (Foucault 1979, 272, 277).

Instead of interpreting this failure as accidental, Foucault points to the social function of the delinquent class: those responsible for crimes against property are isolated. The eighteenth and nineteenth centuries saw rebellion against the laws that legitimated property rights and the power of the emerging economic order. Those responsible for crimes against the bourgeoisie were identified and separated from the populace at large (Foucault 1979, 272–74). The image of the criminal as folk hero began to fade, and the delinquent was regarded as different from the rest of society, as morally or psychologically inferior (Foucault 1979, 275–276). Thus crimes against property were moralized and separated from political struggle (Foucault 1980b, 41). Although recidivism appeared as a problem with the first prisons, it was a manageable, and even useful side-effect of incarceration. Even if delinquency becomes habitual, it is repeated *as delinquency*, as containable, isolated crimes against property; it is not experienced by the populace as the first stirrings of a mass revolt against the existing economic order. The advantage of the prison was that it created a class of delinquents as an "enclosed illegality." This subclass was now "concentrated, supervised, and disarmed" (Foucault 1979, 278).

Still broader social functions were established with the emergence of the prison. The most salient of these is the political justification for routine surveillance of the population (Foucault 1979, 280–281). Sheridan provides an apt summation of this phenomenon:

> Crimes produced the prison; the prison the delinquent class; the existence of the delinquent class an excuse for the policing of the entire population [Sheridan 1980, 161].

It is important to remember that Foucault does not claim that this analysis of penology provides a universal pattern exactly applicable to the correlation of power and knowledge operative in every discourse. His analysis provides a point of entry, a guiding set of questions; it challenges us to examine the particular configurations of power and knowledge in other discourses.

In applying Foucault's questions to the Christian tradition, my aim is to understand Christianity in terms of its practices, not just in terms of its symbols and doctrines. To examine the power of Christianity, to discern its effects of truth in particular situations, means that the theologian must not limit her or his work to an examination of the internal coherence of doctrines or their correspondence to traditional authoritative sources of theological reflection such as scriptural traditions, the authentic words of Jesus, or the history of church doctrine. Nor do I suggest using Foucault's work as a formula for analyzing the political meaning of symbols and doctrines. I do not find in Foucault ready-made answers to the question of the operation of power in any sort of discourse. He does, however, provide a grid through which various operations of power may be examined.

THE GENEALOGICAL METHOD: SUBJUGATED KNOWLEDGES

Foucault analyzes the power dimensions of discourse in two ways: one method he calls an archaeology; the other, a genealogy. *Archaeology* is the method by which Foucault investigates the production of discourse, its correlation with institutions and systems of order, appropriation, and exclusion. *Genealogy* is the method Foucault uses to examine resistance to dominant forms of power and knowledge.

Foucault focuses on resistance to dominant forms of discourse, describing these resistances as an "insurrection of subjugated knowledges." He identifies the current, ongoing resistance to established discourses as follows:

> . . . it is a fact that we have repeatedly encountered . . . in the course of the most recent times, an entire thematic to the effect that it is not theory but life that matters, not knowledge but reality, not books but money, etc.; but it also seems to me that over and above, and arising out of this thematic, there is something else to which we are witness, and which we might describe as an *insurrection of subjugated knowledges* [Foucault 1980b, 81].

By "subjugated knowledges" Foucault means both a particular event or events, and a particular set of ideas or values. The term "subjugated knowledges" refers to a specific history, the history of subjugation, conflict, and domination, lost in an all-encompassing theoretical framework or erased in a triumphal history of ideas. "Subjugated knowledges" also refers to a whole group of knowledges that have been regarded with disdain by intellectuals as being either primitive or woefully incomplete. These are "naive knowledges, located low down on the hierarchy, beneath the required level of cognition or scientificity" (Foucault 1980b, 81–82).

In both meanings we find a common object—the historical knowledge of struggles:

> In the specialised areas of erudition as in the disqualified, popular knowledge there lay the memory of hostile encounters which even up to this day have been confined to the margins of knowledge [Foucault 1980b, 83].

In subjugated knowledges there is retained the awareness of the constitutive role of conflict in discourse, a role that is avoided in our theories of language and our institutionalizations of discourse. Foucault's genealogical work is directed toward remembering and bringing into active struggle these memories of conflict and power.

Let us give the term *genealogy* to the union of erudite knowledge and local memories which allows us to establish a historical knowledge of struggles and to make use of this knowledge tactically today [Foucault 1980b, 83].

Foucault's genealogies explicitly address a perilous, fearful aspect of discourse, its intrinsic relation to conflict and domination. Genealogy is a mode of investigation appropriate for a theology that understands Christian faith as a commitment to eradicate oppression and to establish justice, and understands theology as the analysis of the conditions and motives of such work for justice.

POWER/KNOWLEDGE

Foucault's analysis of the insurrection of subjugated knowledges, and his attention to the history of conflict within discourse leads to a new formulation of the problems typically grouped under the rubric "theory and practice." Foucault does not understand practice as the application of theory, nor does he operate with "a Marxist understanding which entails a totalization of theory and practice" (Hacking 1981, 32). Foucault addresses the relation of theory and practice in terms of their constitutive relation: politics is constitutive of his own theoretical work, and in his analyses, we discover the constitutive role of politics in other systems of thought. The question of the relation of theory and practice is, for Foucault, a key element in the question of truth.

Foucault addresses the problem of theory and practice—the relation of ideas and political, social, or economic structures—as a problem of the relationship between power and knowledge. What produces our knowledge about the world, our theories? To answer this question Foucault turns to political and social structures. Who is it that knows in a particular society? Whose knowledge is taken as real and whose is rejected as inadequate, either as unscientific or unpious? The relation of power and knowledge also raises other questions. Is knowledge itself powerful? How does knowledge shape political, social, and economic structures?

Through such questions Foucault not only rethinks the relationship between two givens—power and knowledge—but also rethinks the definitions of each of these phenomena. In his review of Foucault's book *Power/ Knowledge*, Hacking describes two conceptions of the relationship between power and knowledge that Foucault wishes to avoid. The first is the simple idea that "knowledge provides an instrument that those in power can use for their own ends." The second is the view that "a new body of knowledge brings into being a new class of people who can exercise a different kind of power.'' These two notions imply ''two correlative concepts about the role of ideology. The first implies that a ruling class generates an ideology that suits its own interests; the second that a new ideology creates space for a new ruling class'' (Hacking 1981, 32).

Foucault's approach to the relation of power and knowledge moves far beyond these simple dichotomies. In his consideration of power, he examines its different levels of operation, its productive as well as its repressive aspects. In retrospect, he identifies his histories of madness, medicine, and the human sciences as being concerned with power, although that point was not explicitly recognized at the time (Foucault 1980b, 115). Foucault's explanation for the lack of clarity about power in his early writing points out the importance of political forces in shaping the aims and results of theoretical work. Foucault gives political reasons for his earlier lack of ''theoretical'' precision, stating that his incapacity to ask about power was related to the way in which that word was used in the struggle between socialists and capitalists.

> I can say that this was an incapacity linked undoubtedly with the political situation we found ourselves in. . . . The way power was exercised —concretely and in detail—with its specificity, its techniques and tactics, was something that no one attempted to understand; they contented themselves with denouncing it in a polemical and global fashion as it existed among the 'others,' in the adversary camp. Where Soviet socialist power was in question, its opponents called it totalitarianism; power in Western capitalism was denounced by the Marxists as class domination; but the mechanics of power in themselves were never analysed [Foucault 1980b, 115–116].

Concern with power and knowledge leads Foucault to a radical critique of the Western ''will to truth,'' a political construction of what counts as true, a political construction that passes as truth in itself. As Colin Gordon states in his afterword to *Power/Knowledge*, to understand and appreciate Foucault one must be able to follow him in his questioning of the order of rationality itself (Gordon 1980, 231). As a feminist theologian of liberation, I find it impossible not to ask similar questions, not to entertain suspicions about the intrinsic imperialism of Western conceptions of the nature of knowledge. With Foucault one questions the Western form of the will to know, its constitutive elements, its correlation with elitism and oppression, and its continuing appropriateness for human survival.

This critical relativism has been noted by other interpreters of Foucault. Rorty grounds it in Foucault's fusion of Nietzsche and Marx. Rorty states that ''through his appropriation of these two philosophers, Foucault offers what people want and expect in a great thinker'':

> A view about what values to place on current knowledge claims, and hints about how to change the world. More specifically, he combines a

sceptical judgement about the nature of science with concrete suggestions about how power might be taken from those who presently possess it [Rorty 1981, 5].

To understand Foucault's analysis of discourse, one must sympathize with the project of investigating rationality itself as always particular, thus examining its history and its contingent forms. Foucault states that the necessity of such an investigation is brought about by sudden changes in certain empirical forms of knowledge, changes that do not follow rhythms of transformation or accepted schemes of development. What happens is both abrupt and radical:

> These are not simply new discoveries, there is a whole new "regime" in discourse and forms of knowledge. . . . This extent and rapidity are only the sign of something else: a modification in the rules of formation of statements which are accepted as scientifically true [Foucault 1980b, 112].

Foucault questions accepted ways of understanding transformation in science, arguing that the changes he has found in certain forms of knowledge cannot be understood merely in terms of a change of content or of theoretical formulation:

> Thus it is not a change of content (refutation of old errors, recovery of old truths), nor is it a change of theoretical forms (renewal of a paradigm, modification of systematic ensembles). It is a question of what governs statements, and the way in which they govern each other so as to constitute a set of propositions which are scientifically acceptable, and hence capable of being verified or falsified by scientific procedures [Foucault 1980b, 112].

This problem of transformation in warrants is referred to as that of the régime of truth, the politics of the scientific statement. In order to investigate this problem of power and knowledge, the determinations of what counts as knowable or true, one is asked to follow Foucault in the pursuit of four basic questions. These questions are described by Colin Gordon as follows:

> (1) A "genealogical" question: what kind of political relevance can enquiries into our past have in making intelligible the "objective conditions" of our social present, not only its visible crises and fissures but also the solidity of its unquestioned relations?
>
> (2) An "archaeological" question: how can the production in our societies of sanctioned forms of rational discourse be analysed according to their material, historical conditions of possibility and their governing systems of order, appropriation, and exclusion?

(3) An "ethical" question: what kind of relations can the role and activity of the intellectual establish between theoretical research, speialised knowledge, and political struggles?

(4) Lastly, a further question fundamental to the possibility of analysing the preceding ones, the question of the proper use to be made of the concept of power, and of the mutual enwrapping, interaction, and interdependence of power and knowledge [Gordon 1980, 233].

A THEOLOGY OF RESISTANCE

There is a striking convergence in the work of Michel Foucault and the concerns of liberation theologians. Foucault's work complements that done by liberation theologians in two ways. First, Foucault is aware of the repressive role of ostensibly liberating forms of discourse. His awareness is akin to that which inspires liberation theologians' critiques of academic Western theology and of standard economic and political policies of development. Second, Foucault is committed to challenging oppression (he writes of the insurrection of subjugated knowledges) and is thoroughly self-critical. However, one does not find in Foucault pretensions to a definitive political program or an exclusive perspective capable of disclosing the secrets of society and history. It is the paradoxical or dialectical element in Foucault that makes his work especially suggestive for a theology done from the perspective of one who is both oppressor and oppressed. Foucault combines struggle against oppression with awareness of the partiality of that struggle and the analyses that derive from it. As Foucault so provocatively states in an interview:

. . . I am well aware that I have never written anything but fictions. . . . One "fictions" history on the basis of a political reality that makes it true, one "fictions" a politics not yet in existence on the basis of a historical truth [Foucault 1980b, 193].

The combination of relativism with resistance to particular configurations of power/knowledge marks the strength and uniqueness of Foucault's critique. This juxtaposition of relativism and critique is cogently expressed as follows:

It's not a matter of emancipating truth from every system of power (which would be a chimera, for truth is already power) but of detaching the power of truth from the forms of hegemony, social, economic, and cultural, within which it operates at the present time [Foucault 1980b, 133].

For one suspicious of the scientific claims of Marxist critiques, or suspicious of any claims to have discovered the essence of Christianity, Foucault's thoroughgoing relativism offers a style of thought that is both critical of oppression and yet continuously self-critical.

Transformation of the Western Theological Episteme

Examining liberation theology and my work in a feminist theology of liberation through the lens of Foucault's genealogy and archaeology of knowledge, it becomes apparent that such theologies are not merely variants within theology but may represent a new episteme. The warrants and truth-claims of these theologies diverge sharply from those of traditional theology.

For liberation theologians, the truth of Christian faith is not an abstract or universal description of the God-human relationship but is intrinsically historical and practical. Gutiérrez describes the task of liberation theology in these terms:

> . . . the theology of liberation offers us not so much a new theme for reflection as a *new way* to do theology. Theology as critical reflection on historical praxis is a liberating theology. . . . This is a theology which does not stop with reflecting on the world, but rather tries to be part of the process through which the world is transformed [Gutiérrez 1973, 15].

Another liberation theologian, Jon Sobrino, makes a similar point, arguing that the shift in theological perspective involves a change in the adjudication of theological claims from the realm of theory to that of practice. He discusses this specifically in reference to the question of theodicy:

> Yet Latin American theodicy has peculiar features of its own insofar as liberation theology arose out of active praxis rather than static contemplation. Faced with a pervasive situation of misery, it does not take the classic tack to be found in the Book of Job, in the work of Dostoyevsky, and more recently in Rabbi Rubinstein's query as to how Jews can believe in God after Auschwitz. It is not concerned with finding some way to contemplate God and captivity in a meaningful relationship . . . it is inspired and sustained by the conviction that the real problem is not to justify God but rather to turn the justification of human being into a reality . . . the quandary of theodicy must be resolved in praxis rather than in theory [Sobrino 1978, 36].

Dorothee Soelle provides a concise statement of the same point: "From a Christian point of view, theory and praxis can be understood today only in their unity, which means truth is not something that we find or by which we are found, but something that we make true" (Soelle 1974, 77). The corresponding warrant for theological reflection is also practical:

The truth of Christ exists only as concrete realization, which means: the verification principle of every theological statement is the praxis that it enables for the future. Theological statements contain as much truth as they deliver practically in transforming reality [Soelle 1974, 76].

To take liberation theology at its most radical is to recognize it as the formulation of a political understanding of truth and theory. Thus, to ask liberation theologians to answer ontological or metaphysical questions is to ask them no longer to do liberation theology. Those questions may still be asked by traditional thinkers. Liberation theology, however, represents a different focus, and to attempt to find in it an ontology or a universal anthropology is to miss the point of its innovation: the operation of a practical, not a speculative, concept of truth.

In turning to the actuality of liberation, to practice as the primary criterion for theological reflection, I find myself distanced from traditional theology in yet another sense. To use scripture and the person and work of Jesus as criteria for faith and theological reflection, while definitely more particular than to use ontological structures as points of evaluation, is still to avoid the costs and risks of history. I will not ground a feminist theology of liberation in either scripture or in the person and work of Jesus. To do either would be to abdicate liberation theology's uniqueness: its reconceptualization of theology in light of a particular experience of the relation between theory and practice. Feminist theology is grounded in the liberating experience of sisterhood, in the process of liberation from sexism; Latin American theologies of liberation are grounded in the resistance and solidarity within base Christian communities.

I have learned from other liberation theologians the importance of the correlation between theory and practice, between faith and the transformation of social structures. Although I follow this reconceptualization, working in my particular situation as both oppressor and oppressed has led me to conclusions different from those of black theologians of liberation and Latin American theologians of liberation. The difference lies primarily in our relation to the Christian tradition and in our interpretation of the claim that it is, in some way, "true." In the following pages, I will analyze the strand of liberation theology that I have chosen to develop: the practical concept of truth. I will not attempt an exploration of liberation theology's reliance on the authority of tradition and of scripture, but merely present my reasons for avoiding those authorities.

Although we differ in our choice of sources, I am still indebted to liberation theologians. I have found significant elements of their work challenging and fruitful. One of these elements is the open and consistent commitment to solidarity with the oppressed, which is evident even in their definition of the theological task. Liberation theologians are most consistent in their reliance on practice as the matrix and criterion of theological reflection when the aim of their work is not the production of new systems but the maintenance of an open process of reflection and social and individual formation. The primary content of liberation theologies—the description of a community's struggle for transformation in response to the ideal of solidarity—is more properly understood as a method, a process of inclusiveness and of focus on specific historical structures of existence. Liberation theology does not present a well-defined concept of the nature of human being and human community as such.

Liberation theology, as it now exists, is like the work of the later Foucault in its explicit identification with the perspective of the oppressed. Liberation theologians are even more forthright about this than is Foucault. They state repeatedly that their work can only be understood within the horizon of an a priori commitment to the oppressed. Chastised by Foucault's critique of the power and peril of discourse, I maintain this perspective but do so with a note of skepticism. I agree that it is important to identify one's perspective and to choose to enter the "battle for truth" on the side of the oppressed, yet I do so for reasons different from those given by some liberation theologians. Rather than grounding this choice in some atemporal or noncontingent structure—tradition, revelation, the person and work of Jesus—I understand this choice to be a moral one, a choice not free from the concomitant element of risk.

Epistemological Privilege of the Oppressed

In light of Foucault's analysis of discourse, I believe the choice of a particular locus of reflection is extremely important, and the importance of the choice is directly correlative with its uncertainty. In liberation theology one chooses to think and act from the perspective of the oppressed. I believe that this option is chosen, not imposed. To be a feminist theologian of liberation is to recognize the constitutive role of one's matrix—participation in resistance struggles—and to choose to continue to think and act from this perspective, recognizing the contingency of that choice, the possibility of that perspective being superseded.

The choice of perspective determines the nature of liberation theology and of a feminist theology of liberation. The context of these theologies is one stratum within the whole Christian tradition, a particular option that is critical of society and of the institutional church. This stratum is a practical, communal, revolutionary form of ecclesia. Theologies of liberation are rooted in the memory of the revolutionary struggles and hopes expressed in the "underground Bible" and the history of heresies.[2] They are rooted in communities of faith that are continuous with those aspects of the Christian tradition that have been committed to liberation within history and to solidarity with the oppressed.

The content of these theologies is unique, focusing on the theme of solidarity and a concept of a God who evokes conversion to the other. When understood simply as universals, the concepts of God and of solidarity are empty. These concepts are only proleptically universal, evoking particular forms of liberation and resistance in hope—not with certain knowledge—that there is a God who liberates and that liberation may at some time be achieved. The impact of God on human life is similarly historical; it is the evocation of an attitude of sympathy that leads to the critique of particular forms of domination and to the attempt to create new forms of community that are in accord with the fundamental project of solidarity with all people.

Within these theologies, the focus of Christian faith seems more circumscribed than it is in traditional theology. The Christian faith (with its promise and experience of redemption) is pertinent not in regard to the human in itself, but in reference to the human as sinner. And there is even a further delimitation in these communities of faith and their correlative theologies. Their concern is not sin in a universal sense, but sin in particular, sin as the denial of solidarity. A liberating Christian faith addresses historical conditions of fallenness with a hope for and a struggle toward redemption in history. The faith that grounds theologies of liberation is intrinsically historical and particular, directed toward the denunciation and transformation of specific forms of oppression.

Segundo describes this circumscribed or particular focus as the freedom of faith for ideologies, meaning, in a sense of the term peculiar to him, particular projects of liberation. He claims that faith is a process of learning to learn:

> However lofty it may be, it [faith] is ever in the service of historical solutions to human problems—even though the latter solutions will always be provisional and incomplete. Faith, then, is a liberative process. It is converted into freedom for history, which means freedom for ideologies.[3]

If a feminist theology of liberation is understood as a particular option taken in the battle for truth, it is important to maintain its critical function and avoid being co-opted by dominant, oppressive modes of thought. To be historical, one must avoid the bad faith of grounding one's criticisms in ahistorical absolutes. For a theology of liberation, this would take the form of grounding the validity of our insights in privileged representations, arguing that simply because an insight is made from the perspective of the oppressed or is Christian that it is true. I have chosen an alternative to that option. The alternative is to remain open, to understand the validity of my perspective not in terms of some a priori element of human being but in terms of practice, the actual occurrence of social and political emancipation.

The Politics of Universal Discourse

The importance of maintaining openness can be seen through a critique of the alternate stance. I find that Foucault's arguments about the nature of discourse constitute such a persuasive critique. He claims that the search for certainty is itself political, that it represents an attempt to avoid the risk of continued discourse. Foucault argues that the attempt to ground one's political action or understanding of human community in any form of necessity, either that of the structure of human being or of a teleology of history, is itself a political act, an effort to insure the domination of a particular, contingent human project.

> What is that fear which makes you reply in terms of consciousness when someone talks to you about a practice, its conditions, its rules, and its historical transformations? What is the fear which makes you seek beyond all boundaries, ruptures, shifts, and divisions, the great historico-transcendental destiny of the occident? It seems to me that the only reply to this question is a political one [Foucault 1976, 209–210].

The search for the "great historico-transcendental destiny of the occident" is as characteristic of Western theology as it is of Western philosophy. Traditional theologians such as Rahner, Tillich, and Barth claim that their work is an expression of something that is universally true of all human beings. There are several dimensions to the repressive political function of this type of theological work. Liberation theologians claim that by focusing on the universal rather than the particular, traditional theology trivializes human suffering in history (Metz 1980, 65). They argue that traditional theology—in contrast to their attempts to maintain the dangerous memory of suffering—has tended to leave the concrete reality of oppression and destruction unchallenged (Metz 1980, 115, 100–118).

Traditional theology is also criticized by liberation theologians as being falsely universal, claiming to speak for the human as such, but ignoring the experience of minorities and women of all races. James Cone sharply criticizes this dimension of traditional theology:

> Unfortunately not only white seminary professors but some blacks as well have convinced themselves that only the white experience provides the appropriate context for questions and answers concerning things divine. They do not recognize the narrowness of their experience and the particularity of their theological expressions. They like to think of themselves as *universal* people. . . . They fail to recognize that other people also have thought about God and have something significant to say about Jesus' presence in the world [Cone 1975, 14–15].

Traditional theology can be criticized on further grounds. It is a type of self-securing, a flight from the peril of discourse that is always contingent, particular, and frighteningly powerful. This flight results in the deadliness of discourse that, in order to maintain its primacy or universality, excludes as particular modifications or as trivial any experience that would challenge its interpretation. A striking example of this danger is the apparent obliviousness to the experience of women in much liberal theology. Feminist theologians such as Valerie Saiving and Judith Plaskow argue, for example, that traditional theologians have understood sin in terms of male experience. Challenges to that understanding and alternative interpretations of the nature of sin from the experience of women are regarded as either unnecessary or as particular modifications of the universal structure of fallenness, which can be ascertained from male experience alone (Saiving 1979, 27; Plaskow 1980).

The Power and Peril of Theological Discourse

For liberation theology to remain critical, liberation theologians must remember that we, too, share in the power and peril of discourse. I find that the difficulties of discourse as analyzed by Foucault apply all too well to theological discourse. Theology shares the "anxiety as to just what discourse is, when it is manifested materially, as a written or spoken object" (Foucault 1976, 216). The nineteenth and twentieth centuries are replete with examinations of the nature of theological language, with different formulations of the basis and status of its claims. There are many options, from attempts to interpret theological language within an analytical framework to expositions of it as essentially narrative, metaphorical, or imaginative.

Theology shares in another aspect of the peril of discourse; the uncertainty occasioned by its transitory nature. Foucault describes this as the awareness that discourse is "destined for oblivion," that it participates in a temporality that we can neither control nor predict (Foucault 1976, 216). The oblivion of earlier discourses, the strange pattern of change within the Christian tradition, is a symptom of this temporality. Conflict and change, far from being transitory aspects of the Christian tradition, appear to have characterized it from its origins. Ernst Käsemann, for example, claims that the variability of theological positions in early Christianity was so great that the New Testament canon does not constitute the foundation for the unity of the Christian church but is rather the basis for the multiplicity of confessions (Käsemann 1971, 66; Harrington 1971, 247, 369).

While the temporality of discourse and uncertainty as to its nature are unsettling, this dis-ease is compounded by an awareness of the power of this fragile and disturbingly contingent phenomenon. Foucault reminds us of "the uncertainty at the suggestion of barely imaginable powers and dangers behind this activity, however humdrum and grey it may seem" (Foucault 1976, 216). This is a reminder that although it is contingent and transitory, discourse has effects of truth. What we say may not last, and we may not understand its relation to "reality," but it does matter. Discourse does, in some complex way, shape our world. The same is true of theology. The ways in which we understand the nature of faith and ecclesia are not irrelevant. These understandings have life and death consequences; they determine the type of response the church makes to particular social and political crises; they shape the nature of human community and human belonging in the world.

Another dimension of the fear of discourse is also relevant to theology. It is the fear most explicitly thematized by liberation theologians: the "uncertainty faced when we suspect the conflicts, triumphs, injuries, dominations and enslavements that lie behind these words, even when long use has chipped away their rough edges" (Foucault 1976, 216). Daly and Cone are among those who have exposed this dimension of theological discourse, the conflicts and dominations that lie behind the victory of orthodoxy.[4]

James Cone denounces the correlation between theological positions and racism, arguing that both conservative and liberal theologians miss "the decisive ingredient of the gospel message—the liberation of the oppressed from sociopolitical humiliation for a new freedom in Christ" (Cone 1975, 51). He castigates those who defended slavery in the eighteenth and nineteenth centuries and claims that these attitudes are still represented in conservative churches and seminaries. Cone states that a view of the gospel that does not challenge racism as inherently unchristian "is not arrived at through an open encounter with the biblical message, but is exclusively determined by the continued social and political dominance of whites over blacks" (Cone 1975, 50).

Mary Daly discloses the form of domination that eliminated female traditions of knowing by actually murdering women during the church-supported witch-craze of the fifteenth, sixteenth, and seventeenth centuries.

> . . . the christians will[ed] to destroy real female-identified goodness, that is, the independence, strength, wisdom and learning through which Hags (healers, counselors, wise women, teachers) earned the respect of the people. . . . the victimizers belonged to a "higher" class of men, in the sense that they had professional legitimation and *officially recognized* knowledge. If we examine the status of the victims, it is clear that these women . . . constituted a threat to the rising professional hierarchy precisely as possessors of (unlegitimated) higher learning, that is, of spiritual wisdom and healing and of the highly independent character that accompanies such wisdom [Daly 1978, 193, 195].

The Practice of Truth

Sensitivity to the power and peril of discourse, remembrance of the domination of women of all races, people of color, and the poor by learned philosophers and theologians, leads to an alternative concept of truth. Thinking within the horizon of these conflicts also leads to a note of tenuousness and skepticism. As a feminist I need skepticism because of the experience of having universes of meaning shattered, of recognizing that what I had accepted as true—definitions of human nature, the roles of women and men, the appropriate language for deity—was created within unnecessary relations of power and domination. The outcome of such shifts in my thinking is continual self-suspicion. I can no longer trust my feelings of certainty once basic myths and ideals have been exposed as illusory and ideological. Even a feeling of certainty is contingent; it is only a sign of participation in a particular episteme.

The feeling of suspicion is not unique either to myself or to feminists. It is also discussed by such philosophers as Richard Rorty. In his work I find a helpful discussion of a concept of truth that is correlative with such suspicion. Rorty claims that rather than seeking to avoid error through finding certain or unquestionable foundations of knowledge, it is possible to avoid error by maintaining openness in the ongoing conversation and struggle for truth (Rorty 1979, 373–379). My work and liberation theology both present a similar yet more defined claim than Rorty's. Openness in theological discourse is a concomitant of commitment to the oppressed, commitment to the importance of the perspective of those people and groups who are marginal and exploited. Solidarity with these people prevents a too early foreclosure of discourse.

It is important to remember that even this methodological criterion— openness to the perspective of the oppressed—represents a choice. It is not the only way of defining and determining the truth of discourse. We have reasons for making this choice, but the choice is not forced by them. The arena of adjudication of this choice is not correlation with some objective reality that confronts us but is itself practical. The value of this choice is demonstrated only in its implementation, in the creation of a politics of truth that defines the true as that which liberates and furthers specific processes of liberation.

A theology of liberation is part of the work for a certain type of human community, one in which freedom is possible, one always aware of the historical and material threats to the human sociality and existence that it values. Liberation theologians are not concerned with the essence of human being *per se*, but with the creation or maintenance of a specific *form* of human existence. In our work for communities of justice and peace, it is crucial that we remember how easily structures of sisterhood and brotherhood are obliterated. The obliteration of any feeling of solidarity between the victims and the oppressors within the death camps at Auschwitz, the denial of solidarity in the Gulag, and the ongoing denial of solidarity in the torture of political prisoners—all these serve as painful reminders of the fragility and unnecessary status of the ideals of human dignity and solidarity.

3

Dangerous Memory and Alternate Knowledges

The power and peril of discourse and the constant tendency to elide its pitfalls characterize theology as much as they do the discourse of penology, sexuality, and madness. Within the Christian tradition, radically different understandings of the nature of God, of faith, of sin and redemption are produced by people who rely on the same sources: scripture, doctrine, tradition, and the contemporary life of faith. Some Christian theologians claim that such endless changes in theological discourse can be avoided. They find a secure home for theological discourse in ahistorical or supernatural authorities, either in revelation as found in scripture and doctrine or in the weight and wisdom of tradition. Both authorities are valued and used without acknowledgment that they are characterized by the same tenuousness, contingency, and partiality as the discourse they are presumed to ground.[1]

The methodological difficulties in theology are not often described as part of an elision of discourse. Yet I find in theology signs of such an elision, signs of unease as to the nature of theology, the type of truth-claims it can make, the warrants that establish its importance, the realm to which it refers. These questions do not only stem from the plurality of theologies, each with a different understanding of its status in relation to faith and to other disciplines. Christian theology has been characterized by plurality since its inception. While this plurality of options may not be greater now than at any other time in the past, the self-evidence of theology as a discrete if debatable method with an identifiable or meaningful referent has been shattered (Käsemann 1964, 100).

The nineteenth and twentieth centuries have reflected this "dis-ease" of theology, the loss of an obvious referent and method. As the "death of God"—the lost of an absolute referent as constitutive of human existence—permeated much of Western culture, theology sought either to accommodate itself to secularity by interpreting it as coherent with incarnational faith or to oppose it with a neo-orthodox positivism of revelation.

32

The "shaking of the foundations" has not stopped, however, with the shaking of the foundations of Christian theism (Tillich 1950). The twentieth century could just as well be characterized by the shaking of the foundations of humanism and secularity: the increasing fragility of the morality of humanity and of technological, scientific society as manifest in the Nazi holocaust, the nuclear arms race, genocide, poverty, ecological disasters, and the exploitation of scarce resources. As the old certitudes, the old gods, crumble, new ones have risen to take their place: national socialism in Nazi Germany, the "Christo-fascism" of the moral majority in the United States (Soelle 1983, 19), the ideology of the national security state. Our era is marked as much by the struggle of competing gods as it is by the death of God.

In the midst of this confusion, the increasingly strong voice of liberation theology, a specific form of ecclesiality and reflection, declares that the problem with Christendom is not that its claims were false or unrealistic, but that it failed to claim enough, to hope enough. Liberation theology is a proclamation of the presence of the God of Exodus, the God of liberation. It is an impassioned critique of society and established religion and theology in the name of justice. Liberation theology exposes the conflictual fabric of traditional Western academic theology; it is forging a new type of discourse that struggles for truth within that power- and ideology-ridden matrix.

COMMUNITIES OF RESISTANCE

The significance of liberation theology lies in its matrix and its content. Its matrix is that of the "*battle* for truth," not just the proclamation of revealed truths. Metz, for example, speaks of the crisis of faith as practical, not intellectual. The fundamental failure of Christianity, as he sees it, is not its inability to deal with the philosophical critiques of theological knowledge offered by the Enlightenment. The failure of Christianity is a failure of practice, a failure to transform the corruption and inhumanity of the world. The failure of Christendom is not a failure of intellectual understanding, but a failure to establish in practice its vision of the human community (Metz 1980, 75–76).

The critique of Christendom by liberation theologians emerges from a specific matrix: the struggle to establish as true in history what has been declared from the perspective of faith as the truth of human being in the world. Liberation theology is not based in the academy, in the study of texts or a specific literature; it is based in actual communities in the concrete experience of women and men struggling to build a new world. Their vision of this new world is forged in the context of a community of faith, a community that appropriates the Christian tradition in the context of political and social struggle.

There is yet another aspect of this matrix that is central to understanding the significance of liberation theologies. The most vital expressions of liberation theology have come from the fringes of the Christian tradition. The primary source for liberation theology is not the intellectual or scholarly theological tradition, but the experience of those who have been excluded from structures of power within society and within the church. Liberation theologians express the voice and experience of women of all races, racial and ethnic minorities, and the poor of the Third World.

The terms used by liberation theologians often belie the revolutionary significance of their knowledge. Their language is that of traditional theology— God, Christ, salvation, sin, grace—but the meanings of these traditional terms are distinctly nontraditional. Liberation theology uses the same symbols that are found in traditional theology, but they are interpreted by different criteria. There may still be exegesis, apologetics, and dogmatics within liberation theology, but these traditional tasks are all performed within a different horizon—that of resistance to oppression. Merely to state that liberation theology is reflection on practice is to obscure this horizon and to overlook the epistemic shift constitutive of this theology. The reflection of liberation theologians on practice entails a reconsideration of the nature of theological reflection and the identification of a particular sort of practice— resistance to oppression—as the focus of Christian faith and theology.

My claims for liberation theology may appear extravagant. Although the movement is coextensive with a radical or revolutionary political option, and is thus quite different from mainstream Christianity and its politics, it is possible to miss the epistemic challenge of liberation theology. The reason for this is found in the explanations given by liberation theologians themselves of their work. While the constitutive role of practice and commitment to the oppressed is central, many liberation theologians also claim as warrant for their theological work a traditional source: the revelation of God as found in scripture.

Biblical traditions are important for liberation theologians; study of the scriptures is a central feature of base Christian communities and funds the powerful imagery of preaching in the black church. The political interpretation of their faith cannot, however, be explained solely by the impact of biblical texts. How can the same collection of texts be used to support both a political and an ostensibly apolitical church? I think that the answer lies in who is reading the texts, what community is providing, as Sharon Parks puts it, the point of reference.[2] The determining factor in shaping liberation faith and theology is not the scriptures in themselves, but who is reading the scriptures and why.

Locating the fundamental source of liberation theology in communities of and for the oppressed is of special importance in my work as a feminist theologian of liberation, but it is not totally foreign to the work of other liberation theologians. I do not think that liberation theology offers us the finally definitive reading of the scriptures. What it offers is something that is both more modest and more revolutionary: an interpretation of scriptural traditions (and thus of human being, of history, and of political structures) by those who have not yet named the world—the marginal, the silenced, the defeated.

A GENEALOGY OF RESISTANCE

What follows is both an exposition and an extension of liberation theology and its definition of truth; it is descriptive and constructive. I describe some of the present tendencies of liberation theologians and I construct a method of reflection, a strategy in the battle for truth, that reflects my own social location—white, Western, feminist, middle-class.

Liberation theology is an insurrection of subjugated knowledges and the manifestation of a new episteme.[3] Liberation theology is grounded in a particular activity of the church, not in an exegesis of scripture, in an interpretation of the Christian tradition, or in philosophical questions and concerns. The basis of my reflection is not only the present life of the church, but it is a particular type of church, one that follows not denominational but political divisions. Liberation theology is grounded in churches of and for the oppressed; thus its basis is an explicitly politicized church. This church consists of communities of faith that challenge the existing order of society as being institutionally repressive and unjust.

We find here three ways of identifying liberation theology. It is a theology of and for the present: the present needs of humanity are its primary focus, determining problems addressed and answers given. It is a theology of the church: the activity of ecclesia is its primary source. And, it arises from a particular type of ecclesia, one which identifies with the needs of an oppressed group and struggles to end their oppression.

These elements of liberation theology can be more explicitly identified and methodologically elaborated when the method of liberation theology is understood as a genealogy of subjugated knowledges. To identify liberation theology explicitly as an insurrection of subjugated knowledges provides us with a rationale for its central themes: a pretheoretical commitment to the oppressed as the focus of theological reflection and a turn to the practical category of liberation as the criterion of "authentic" Christianity and evidence of the truth of Christianity.

To state that liberation theology is an insurrection of subjugated knowledges means that the discourse of liberation theology represents the resurgence of knowledges suppressed by a dominant theology and a dominant culture. Further analysis involves three elements of genealogy: (1) the preservation and communication of memories of conflict and exclusion; (2) the discovery and exposition of excluded contents and meanings; and (3) the strategic struggle between the subjugated and dominant knowledges (Foucault 1980b, 81–83).

DANGEROUS MEMORY

Like Foucault's genealogies, liberation theology begins with the fact of insurrection, not with an abstract or normative statement that there should be resistance. It begins by recognizing actual challenges to repressive aspects of society and of the institutional church and its theology. Metz describes this aspect of theology as the dangerous memory of conflict and exclusion, and he examines the role of the church as the vehicle of that memory (Metz 1980, 66–67).

The Memory of Suffering

Dangerous memory has two dimensions, that of hope and that of suffering. A striking characteristic of liberation theology is its focus on the memory of suffering. Liberation theology recounts the history of the marginal, the vanquished, and the oppressed. Black theology delineates the meaning of salvation and of a God of love and freedom within the matrix of the denial of freedom to black people, within the matrix of a history of dehumanization through slavery, racism, and repression. James Cone describes the perspective of black theology as follows:

In all roles the theologian is committed to that form of existence arising from Jesus' life, death, and resurrection. He knows that the death of the man on the tree has radical implications for those who are enslaved, lynched, and ghettoized in the name of God and country. In order to do theology from that standpoint, he must ask the right questions. . . . The right questions are always related to the basic question: What has the gospel to do with the oppressed of the land and their struggle for liberation? [Cone 1975, 9].

Liberation theology does not address the problem of suffering and evil in the abstract, but focuses on concrete memories of specific histories of oppression and suffering. It declares that such suffering matters; the oppression of people is of ultimate concern. Cone points, therefore, to the ultimate significance of racism, arguing that the issue of racism in our time is analogous to the Arian controversy of the fourth century.

Athanasius perceived quite clearly that if Arius' views were tolerated, Christianity would be lost. But few white churchmen have questioned whether racism was a similar denial of Jesus Christ [Cone 1969, 73].

By placing the issue of racism in the forefront, Cone affirms the significance of a particular history of oppression, and demands that the church confront it explicitly. He claims that "racism implies the absence of fellowship and service, which are primary qualities, indispensable marks of the Church. To be racist is to fall outside the definition of the Church" (Cone 1969, 73).

Black theologians protest the exclusion of black experience from theology and from the life of the church. They claim that the gospel requires the vindication of the poor, the oppressed, and the helpless in society. Black theology is the voice of a particular type of oppression ignored in Western academic theology and in the established churches.

Similar resurgences of particular histories of oppression provide the motive force for the work of both feminist and Latin American theologians. Daly, Ruether, Collins, and Russell denounce the degradation of women in the established churches. They expose the history of women's exclusion from speaking in the church, their exclusion from participation in theology. They challenge traditional definitions of women as evil or weak, definitions that deny the full humanity of women. They trace the history of women's subjugation throughout the Christian tradition, from the misogyny of Genesis through the silencing of women in the early Christian church and the burning of millions of women as witches during the fifteenth, sixteenth, and seventeenth centuries to Barth's definition of women's secondary role in the order of creation. The memory of the church's mutilation, execution, and denigration of women is preserved and exposed by feminist theologians (Daly 1973; Collins 1974; Ruether 1975).

The liberation theology done by Latin American theologians is another expression of a dangerous memory of suffering and oppression. The basis of this theology is the identification of part of the church with the poorest and least powerful segments of society—peasants and Indians. The church of the oppressed serves as their vehicle of protest against an economic situation that concentrates wealth in a small percentage of the population and condemns the majority of the people to poverty.

Latin American liberation theologians assert that the suffering of the poor is an indictment of existing economic and political systems (see Gutiérrez 1973; Míguez 1974; Miranda 1974; Sobrino 1978). Gutiérrez's theology of liberation contains an extensive critique of the policy of economic development implemented in Latin America by the United States (Gutiérrez 1973, 22–42, 81–99, 287–306). Miranda also criticizes the capitalist system of private property because of its contribution to the suffering of the poor (Miranda 1974, 1–33). Archbishop Romero and many other people of faith have been killed because of their determination to name the suffering around them—to be, in Romero's words, the voice of the voiceless (Lernoux 1982).

Memory as Critique

Liberation theology is based on dangerous memories; it recounts the history of human suffering. These accounts of specific histories of oppression are both descriptions and critiques. They serve as critiques of existing institutions and social structures in two ways. First, they criticize the structure of a society and expose its fallacious claim of universality. A society's claim that its economic or political system represents the interests of all people is discredited by the disclosure of who pays the costs of that system and of the imbalance of benefits and costs. The memory of suffering reminds us that, all too often, economic and political systems benefit the few at the cost of the suffering of many others.

Second, the accounts of oppression criticize Western theology and established religion for their failure to address grave human problems, the problems of racism, sexism, and class struggle. By uncovering the suffering unaddressed and thus tacitly tolerated by established religion, liberation theologians criticize the universal pretensions of that religion and expose it as a religion of and for the middle class. Liberation theologians criticize both the rituals and theologies of middle-class religion, seeing in each an avoidance of concrete forms of human suffering. To proclaim and celebrate in liturgy the reconciliation between God and humanity accomplished in the life of Jesus while ignoring the lack of reconciliation between landowners and peasants, between military and Indians is to deny the ongoing power of the gospel to transform human life.

Just as social problems (such as the torture in many Latin American countries) are not acknowledged in traditional liturgies, so academic theology regards the analysis of such problems as secondary. Its primary task is the disclosure of the universals of faith and their correlation with the ontological structure of existence. The limitation of such an ontological analysis is twofold: specific historical concerns are bracketed, and the experience of certain groups of people is excluded from contributing to or determining that analysis. The first limitation is one of time and focus. The task of theological anthropology is to try to understand the nature of the human as such, the possibility of meaning, and the structures of being that underlie particular manifestations of human life such as justice, injustice, and equality. Liberation theologians challenge philosophical or fundamental theology to show the relevance of this sort of investigation to the life and death problems disclosed in the history of human suffering. This is not to say that such work could never be justified, but only that its value can no longer be considered self-evident.

The second limitation of ontological analysis is that it is based solely in the experience of men of a certain class. Those who write and study theology have been predominantly male and middle-class. Men from lower social strata and women lack the access to education needed to engage in the examination of universal or ontological structures of existence and human being. The only basis for that work has been, therefore, a race-, class-, and sex-specific one.

An emphasis on the history of human suffering leads to the declaration that the experience of these people, an experience of the denial and destruction of their humanity, is as normative for our understanding of humanity as is the experience of the victors in historical struggles. The disclosure of the class-, sex-, and race-specific nature of theology is dangerous in that it protests the arrogance, the pretension of men to speak for all humanity and to attempt to ascertain from their limited basis anything universal about human being.

Another dimension of liberation theologians' critique of society and of religion is their exposure of the disparity between discursive and nondiscursive elements in a culture. They contrast the claim of a social system or religion as expressed in literature, philosophy, and theology (the discursive elements) with the concrete relations of power (the nondiscursive elements) in the social system. An example is the contrast between America's ideals of equality and justice and its continuing practice of racism. A similar example comes from feminist theologians, who point out the juxtaposition of the Renaissance claim to humanitarian ideals and to rationality and the simultaneous social practice of witch-burning (Ruether 1975, 89–114; Daly 1978, 178–222).

Critical histories disclose the nonnecessity of the dominant apparatuses of a social system, expose their fragility, and claim that they are attained and maintained only through exclusion and repression. To point to the history of the witch-burnings is to indicate that the silence of women in the church, in medicine, and in the sciences is not a matter of natural law but a matter of the exercise of domination, a power struggle in which women were forcibly excluded.

Similarly, the disclosure of the peasant massacres in the early twentieth century in El Salvador and of the continued resistance of peasants to the economic system which exploits them demonstrates that a system in which a few enjoy economic prosperity and many are poor is not a natural phenomenon but continues to exist only through repression. Memories of struggle against social systems are dangerous; they are witnesses to protests against an order of things that claims to be natural, self-evident, or inevitable.

The Memory of Freedom and Resistance

The dangerous memory expressed in liberation theology is not only a memory of conflict and exclusion as in Foucault's genealogies. It is also a memory of hope, a memory of freedom and resistance. This memory of hope is a significant element of the experience of resistance not treated explicitly by Foucault in his account of genealogy. In order for there to be resistance and the affirmation that is implied in the preservation of the memory of suffering, there must be an experience that includes some degree of liberation from the devaluation of human life by the dominant apparatuses of power/knowledge. Even to resist implies a modicum of liberation and success. Domination is not absolute as long as there is protest against it.

We must be careful here not to reify the existence of resistance, too easily pointing to an undefeatable stratum in human being that always continues to resist. On the contrary, analyses or descriptions of resistance seem to point to something quite different: the contingency of resistance, its frailty, and the possibility and actuality of its being at times obliterated. The fragility of resistance leads me to consider an element of specific histories of oppression that is often mentioned but rarely explained: the paucity of resistance.

Awareness of the scarcity of resistance can be seen in the search by Marxists for a revolutionary proletariat, for the class that becomes conscious of its oppression and then resists. The Frankfurt philosophers Adorno and Horkheimer despaired of ever finding such a class in the industrial West, and Habermas is still looking for a glimmer of resistance shining through the cracks in advanced capitalism.

Martin Jay has described the failure to find a revolutionary subject in the work of the Frankfurt School. Jay finds greater attention is given to universal structures as the historical situation appears less open to revolutionary developments.

> With the shifting of the Institute's emphasis away from class struggle to the conflict between man [*sic*] and nature, the possibility of a historical subject capable of ushering in the revolutionary age disappeared. That imperative for *praxis*, so much a part of what some might call the Institute's heroic period, was no longer an integral part of its thought [Jay 1973, 279].

A similar tension characterizes the work of Jürgen Habermas. Habermas provides an extensive analysis of the legitimation crisis in advanced capitalism, but is unable to locate a revolutionary subject to take advantage of this crisis (Habermas 1973, 33–94).

Even in current experiences of resistance, those committed to that resistance are painfully aware of how long the domination has prevailed and how rare the moments of resistance have been. One of the most striking features of women's history is that the suppression of women was accepted for so long as self-evident and natural. The history of blacks in America also reflects this pattern; black history is characterized by an ongoing struggle not only against racism but also against defeatism and a negative self-image, the internalization of oppression by the oppressed.

The rarity of explicit resistance does not mean that resistance is not occurring just because there are no visible signs of it. Foucault reminds us of the multifarious nature of power, stating that we should be watchful for manifestations of resistance more subtle than armed rebellion or active withdrawal from an oppressive system. The paucity of resistance in any form cannot be denied, however, and prevents us from too easily locating resistance in the nature of human being as such. Apparently human dignity, the will to freedom, or whatever it is that resists, can be effectively neutralized or actually destroyed in individuals and in groups of people.

Given the rarity of resistance, a careful examination of its conditions is hardly an idle inquiry. What is it in fact that enables people to resist? What are the historical conditions of resistance and liberation? The important consideration for liberation theologians is not the universal or a priori conditions of resistance, but the historical conditions of struggles against domination. One could identify in a regional ontology the nature of human being and its capacity for meaning, decision, and action, indicating the universal ground of resistance without understanding why or how in specific histories those fundamental possibilities are actualized or effaced.

Liberation theology is a preservation of dangerous memory, an account of actual, although rare, instances of resistance and liberation. These accounts are a declaration of the possibility of freedom and justice, and they may be examined in an attempt to understand what enables resistance in specific, historical situations. Experiences of partial liberation, experiences that motivate a continued political struggle for liberation, are discussed at different levels by various theologians. Although the degree of analysis varies, the preservation of a memory of historical, actual liberation is common to all liberation theologies.

Such memories are an affirmation of human dignity. They motivate the political struggle against institutions within society and the church that deny and suppress that dignity. James Cone, for example, describes the liberating impact of Christianity on Afro-American women and men during and after slavery. He states that the religion of a God who affirms the worth of all people was lived despite the ideological interpretations of that religion by those who supported slavery. The black church was the locus of experiences of acceptance, love, and dignity. The power that comes from believing that "God" (that which is ultimate) affirms the importance and value of the lives of slaves prevented black acquiescence to the definition of themselves as subhuman by white slave owners. The various African languages and practices of African religion were suppressed, but the Christian religion served as a vehicle for the memory of suffering. In the church it was possible to voice both despair and the hope for release, a hope grounded in the affirmation already experienced.

> How was it possible for black people to keep their humanity together in the midst of servitude, affirming that the God of Jesus is at work in the world, liberating them from bondage? The record shows clearly that black slaves believed that just as God had delivered Moses and the Israelites from Egyptian bondage, he [*sic*] also will deliver black people from American slavery. . . . That truth . . . came from a liberating encounter with the One who is the Author of black faith and existence [Cone 1975, 11, chaps. 1, 2].

Mary Daly describes the interaction of personal and political liberation in the experience of sisterhood.[4] As women share stories of their own lives, a common experience of oppression and of resistance is recognized. This politicizing gives women the courage to persist in resistance, recognizing that their difficulties have not only an individual basis but a social and political basis as well. Fear of moving beyond accepted definitions of behavior is not definitively allayed, but the experience of self-affirmation and hope that comes from the affirmation and community of sisterhood gives courage and enables creative resistance (Daly 1973, 138, 132–154). I, too, interpret the experience of sisterhood as an experience of resistance and liberation, an affirmation of an identity that is different from that imposed by the dominant patriarchal social structures. The experience of resistance is itself a denial of the necessity of patriarchy; it is a moment of freedom, the power to embody momentarily an alternative identity. This affirmation serves as the ground for political resistance to social structures.

Gutiérrez grounds Latin American liberation theology in a similar phenomenon in the Latin American churches. The basis of Latin American liberation theology is the politicization of peasants. The gospel message and the experience of solidarity in base Christian communities gives the peasants a sense of worth and power that counters the definition imposed on them by the church in the past and by their own governments. Gutiérrez writes that the church politicizes the poor by evangelizing.

> . . . the annunciation of the Gospel, precisely insofar as it is a message of total love, has an inescapable political dimension, because it is addressed to people who live within a fabric of social relationships, which, in our case, keep them in a subhuman condition . . . to conscienticize, to politicize, to make the oppressed person become aware that he [sic] is a man [sic] . . . does challenge that privilege [the privilege of the ruling classes] [Gutiérrez 1973, 270].

Metz describes dangerous memory as the remembrance of the process of becoming subjects in the presence of God (Metz 1980, 67). The memory of subjectivity is carried by some forms of ecclesia and by certain strands of the biblical tradition such as the Exodus tradition and the promises in the gospels of the kingdom of God. The memory is of a community in which people were freed to claim an identity different from that imposed on them. It is both a memory of past liberation and a motivation for further liberation. It is a memory of resistance and of hope for further resistance.

The Bearers of Dangerous Memory

The work of liberation theologians is firmly grounded in the reality of oppression and of resistance to oppression. Foucault and many liberation theologians find the impetus for their work in these specific instances of resistance among the oppressed. Their analyses of power and domination do not emerge from mere intellectual curiosity, but from two sources: the fact of resistance, and their own commitment to the oppressed. The attitude of commitment is pretheoretical, the already-given attitude that alternative interpretations and voices claiming oppression should be heard. The philosopher or theologian of resistance then brings the skills of his or her training in analysis and synthesis to bear on the power relations manifest in oppression. The result can be a corpus of work like that of Foucault: an analysis of the concrete mechanisms of exclusion and domination in medicine, penology, the asylum, sexuality. In theology, commitment and reflection have led to works like those of Gutiérrez, Daly, Heyward, and Cone—works that describe specific histories of oppression, criticize the role of the church and theology in that oppression, and offer alternative interpretations of the gospel and ecclesia.

At this stage there is a tension in the articulation of dangerous memories. Often the oppressed either do not resist or their expressions of resistance are more immediate than reflective, taking the form of direct action and symbolic expression. Base Christian communities, the black church, and women's collectives offer numerous examples. Here the form or expression of resistance is often imagistic rather than analytic. It is an expression of protest, hope, and vision that motivates political action.

In the base Christian communities the study of scripture passages that challenge oppression leads to a critique of existing social, political, and economic arrangements.

> They [members of base Christian communities] read the Bible much as medieval and Reformation radicals read it, as a critical and subversive document. They find in it a God who sides with the poor and with others despised by society; who, at the same time, confronts the social and religious institutions that are the tools of injustice [Ruether 1981, 235].

Black theology conceptualizes direct expressions of hope and protest found in spirituals, sermons, and prayers. James Cone analyzes the power of these expressions of faith in the black community's struggle for liberation.

> But when blacks went to church and experienced the presence of Jesus' Spirit among them, they realized that he bestowed a meaning upon their lives that could not be taken away by white folks. That's why folks at Macedonia sang: "A little talk with Jesus makes it right": not that "white is right," but that God had affirmed the rightness of their existence, the righteousness of their being in the world. That affirmation enabled black people to meet "the Man" on Monday morning and to deal with his dehumanizing presence the remainder of the week, knowing that white folks could not destroy their humanity [Cone 1975, 13].

The critical reflection by intellectuals on the symbolic expression and political action of those who are oppressed includes a recognition of the tension implied in theoretical work: it may be either useless or oppressive. The value of a conceptual analysis of powerful systems of action and symbolic reflection is determined by the role that analysis plays in furthering resistance. Its possible oppressiveness lies in what Foucault calls the indignity of speaking for other people. In a conversation between Deleuze and Foucault, Deleuze states:

In my opinion, you were the first—in your books and in the practical sphere—to teach us something absolutely fundamental: the indignity of speaking for others. We ridiculed representation and said it was finished, but we failed to draw the consequences of this "theoretical" conversion—to appreciate the theoretical fact that only those directly concerned can speak in a practical way on their own behalf [Foucault and Deleuze 1977, 209].

Foucault responds by referring to prisoners and to what happened when they began to speak for themselves:

It is this form of discourse which ultimately matters, a discourse against power, the counter-discourse of prisoners and those we call delinquents —and not a theory *about* delinquency [Foucault and Deleuze 1977, 206, 209].

Gutiérrez recognizes this as well. He sees the value of liberation theology as the opening of theological discourse to include the voices of the oppressed.

But in the last instance we will have an authentic theology of liberation only when the oppressed themselves can freely raise their voice and express themselves directly and creatively in society and in the heart of the people of God, when they themselves "account for the hope," which they bear, when they are the protagonists of their own liberation [Gutiérrez 1973, 307].

Respect for the integrity of those who are oppressed is expressed by liberation theologians both in their willingness to learn from symbolic, immediate expressions of hope and protest and in their providing access to communication systems that enable the oppressed to speak for themselves. The Theology in the Americas association, a group of liberation theologians and activists, for example, sponsors conferences in which the primary speakers are those who are oppressed. Foucault's political work focuses not on reforming prisons according to his genealogy of the prison, but on providing structures that allow prisoners to speak for themselves and to make changes based on their analysis (Foucault 1977, 206, 209). In both liberation theology and the work of Foucault there is an ongoing tension between avoiding the indignity of speaking for the oppressed and attempting to respond to their voices by engaging in social and political critique.

THE INSURRECTION OF SUBJUGATED KNOWLEDGES

What happens when the oppressed speak for themselves? Insurrections of subjugated knowledges bring about new interpretations of Christian symbols and texts, new analyses of social structures, critiques of the institutional structure of the church, and solidarity with others. The combined protest of the oppressed and of liberation theologians against existing formulations of the Christian faith and against social structures is made in the name of solidarity. It is motivated by the solidarity of theologians with the victimized, the marginal, and the forgotten. Theologians evaluate traditions and expressions in light of their impact on their lives and on the lives of the oppressed.

The "truth" of Christianity is also understood in terms of solidarity. Solidarity breaks the bonds of isolated individuality and forgetfulness—the bondage of sin—and enables the creation of community and conversion to the other. The Christian message is interpreted as the hope of universal solidarity and the Christian faith is remembered and celebrated as a vehicle of that solidarity. Gutiérrez describes the transformation in existence that is made possible through a liberating faith:

> A spirituality of liberation will center on a *conversion* to the neighbor, the oppressed person, the exploited social class, the despised race, the dominated country. . . . Conversion means a radical transformation of ourselves. . . . To be converted is to commit oneself to the process of the liberation of the poor and oppressed, to commit oneself lucidly, realistically, and concretely [Gutiérrez 1973, 204–205].

Even transcendence is often described in terms of the bonds of solidarity that extend beyond individual existence, rather than in more traditional categories, such as the transcendence of spirit over history and nature or of the divine over the finite. Within a liberating faith, to be a Christian is to belong to a community that extends beyond the individual, and to find meaning in participation in the affirmation of the struggle for humanity. The hope of resurrection is the hope for the power of solidarity to transform reality, a hope that human identity is found in relation to others, in participation in the formation of a community that transcends us now and after death. Dorothee Soelle reinterprets the meaning of resurrection in this vein, giving it social rather than primarily individualistic value.

> Resurrection is the most encoded symbol of the faith, and it resists decoding. It is the utmost yes to life. . . . The symbol transforms even death into an instrument of life. Different times will attempt different translations of this mystery. While the bourgeois theology emphasized the individual dimension, the new theology . . . will emphasize the social dimension of the mystery. Hence we bring together liberation with resurrection because our deepest need is not personal immortality but a life before death for all human beings [Soelle 1978, 34].

Images of the transcendence of God are also closely correlated with the transcendence of community, with the redemptive power of community and of the gift of solidarity. Miranda, for example, identifies the transcendence of God with the imperative of justice:

> . . . when Jeremiah 31:31–34 says that Yahweh *will* be God, it means that compassion, solidarity, and justice will reign among people. This is why the God of the Bible is a future God: because only in the future, at the end of history, will people recognize in the outcry and the otherness of their neighbor the absolute moral imperative that is God [Miranda 1977, 44].

SOLIDARITY AND PRACTICE

The emphasis on solidarity means more than simply the discovery of another theme for theological reflection. This emphasis marks the manifestation of a new episteme. It implies not only a different interpretation of the Christian tradition but a different way of interpreting: it provides a means of understanding in which practice is both a hermeneutic key and a means of verification. Solidarity is inherently practical, and the thought that comprehends it is also intrinsically related to specific practices.

The theoretical content of liberation theology, the elucidation of the theme of solidarity, is itself the elucidation of a particular practice. Solidarity takes the place of traditional notions of redemption: it is evoked or enabled by the grace of God; it is the evidence and the result of God's incarnation; it is the fulfillment of creation.

The correlation of the theoretical content of liberation theology— solidarity—with practice can be understood in three ways. First, one is aware of solidarity and its centrality only through a particular practice, through participation in the resistance struggles of the oppressed. Thus, solidarity is located in an explicitly circular pattern: it emerges as central only from an already existing identification with the oppressed and it evokes further identification with the oppressed.

Second, solidarity serves as a principle of critique; it is a criterion for assessing the nature of the church and other social institutions. Solidarity is of utmost importance to a particular view of faith and serves as a criterion for examining other institutions. This type of faith could motivate critiques similar to Foucault's analyses of the prison, sexuality, the asylum, and clinical medicine. This faith motivates the critique of institutions that systematically repress or exclude particular groups of people.

Third, solidarity provides impetus for political action. Liberating faith leads to constructive action, to a search for institutional structures that enable the experience of the marginal to be formative of a social system and of culture. Thus, solidarity itself means a particular kind of action, a lifestyle expressive of sympathy for and identification with the victimized.

The close correlation of theological work with a particular practice affects the nature of liberation theology. On the surface, liberation theology may appear to be like traditional theology: it examines the standard themes of redemption, christology, ecclesiology, and the doctrine of God. The difference between liberation theology and traditional theology clearly emerges, however, in the differences in the focus of interpretation and in significant warrants. The focus of liberation theology is not on eternal verities but on strategically important ideas. Themes of redemption and christology are treated only in the context of the struggle for liberation. This means that the ideas, doctrines, and symbols of the Christian faith are understood in terms of their function in the struggle of people for liberation.

Dorothee Soelle claims that Christian faith cannot be understood outside involvement in liberation struggles:

> That God loves all of us and each and every individual is a universal theological truth, which without translation becomes the universal lie. The translation of this proposition is world-transforming praxis [Soelle 1974, 107].

The identification of the truth of faith with world-transforming practice means that theology becomes political theology.

> Political theology is rather a theological hermeneutic, which, in distinction from a theology that interprets reality from an ontological or existentialist point of view, holds open an horizon of interpretation in which politics is understood as the comprehensive and decisive sphere in which Christian truth should become praxis [Soelle 1974, 89].

If we understand theology as political theology we are led to three sorts of theoretical work. These three tasks are implicit in the literature of liberation theology; if explicit, both the critical and the constructive impact of liberation theology would be enhanced. One task is the interpretation of Christian symbols as claims about a potential state of justice and peace, as hopes for a particular type of community. This interpretation can take the form of narrative or of doctrine, either expressing a vision of the type of life aimed for by Christians. Another task appropriate for political theology is the investigation of the practical conditions necessary to realize Christian life, the material conditions for solidarity. A third task is the description of the evidence for solidarity, its verification as expressed in actual instances of solidarity.

Political Analysis of Sin and Redemption

The content of liberation theology is the conceptual and symbolic expression of the life of the revolutionary church. My consideration of specific themes within this theology will only be suggestive. Rather than examine the differences among liberation theologians, I will describe a common theme: the political analysis of sin and redemption.

Sin and redemption are understood in liberation theology to be practical, historical, and collective. Liberation theologians emphasize the collective manifestations of sin. They address ways of life, institutions, and cultures that cause oppression and they denounce these as sinful. They denounce structures of injustice rather than individual acts of injustice. Soelle, for example, analyzes the sinfulness of capitalism, a system in which human beings are alienated from themselves, from nature, and from other people. She states that within industrialized society, sin takes the form of "structural alienation from nature, from ourselves, from our being part of the human family and from our fellows" (Soelle 1978, 21). This type of sinfulness is directly related to capitalism.

> On the personal level, capitalism causes alienation; on the interpersonal level, competition; on the social level, it produces class division; on the international, imperialism and war. . . . We should ask ourselves whether we will opt for the Christian faith or for capitalistic values. This will also be the question for the church in this century [Soelle 1978, 43].

Mary Daly and James Cone also expose collective forms of sin. They point to the sin expressed in racism and sexism: the destruction of community between races and sexes, the limitation of the opportunities of minorities and women, and the perpetuation of the privileges of whites over blacks, of men over women.

These analyses of sin and redemption are historical and political, not ontological. Rather than examine the structure of the human will and its potential for sin or describe the sociality of human existence and the possibility for social deformation of individual lives (thus delineating the ontological roots of complicity in institutional evil), liberation theologians analyze particular forms of oppression. They do not address oppression as such, but challenge specific structures of oppression.

James Cone addresses the history of racism in the United States and points to its continued, although sometimes hidden, pervasiveness.

> . . . racism is so embedded in the heart of American society that few, if any, whites can free themselves from it. . . . *The American White man* [sic] *has always had an easy conscience.* But insofar as white do-gooders tolerate and sponsor racism in their educational institutions, their political, economic, and social structures, their churches, . . . they are directly responsible for racism [Cone 1969, 23–24].

Mary Daly writes similarly about the sinfulness of sexism. She argues that a too quick turn to universals, to the problem of human liberation rather than women's liberation, blinds us to the insidious and pervasive manifestations of this particular form of oppression.

. . . some people, especially academics, attempt to make the problem (sexual caste) disappear by *universalization*. One frequently hears: "But isn't the real problem *human* liberation?" The difficulty with this approach is that the words used may be "true," but when used to avoid confronting the specific problems of sexism they are radically untruthful [Daly 1973, 5–6].

Daly delineates structures of patriarchy, finding what is oppressive, and thus sinful, in structures of our common life that once seemed innocuous, structures such as sex-exclusive language, objective, historical accounts of foot binding and witch burnings, and the demeaning practices of modern medicine (Daly 1978, 1–312).

Liberation theologians like Daly, Cone, and Gutiérrez do not try to discover and describe universal conditions for the possibility of sin; they try to unmask the myriad manifestations of particular forms of sin, particular forms of domination. They contend that this unmasking is necessary given the collective nature of sin. Our participation in structures of oppression is largely unconscious. Our complicity is unwitting and naive. The task of liberation theology is to break the facade of innocence and expose the impact of our social system.

Through this effort Third World theologians present a stinging challenge to the First World. They demand that we recognize the exploitation of the Third World by First World nations. In naming this exploitation as sin, theologians challenge the individualistic, universal concept of sin that prevails in churches in the Western world. This concept of sin has allowed the imbalance of access to material goods to be perpetuated for centuries. Miranda points to the irony of Christian churches' defending private ownership of the means of production, since he sees such economic structures to be in direct conflict with the biblical imperative of justice (Miranda 1974, xvi, 1–33). Metz claims that the defense of an exploitative economic system has been possible because Christianity became a religion of the middle class and did not challenge the values of that class. He examines and criticizes this privatized, trivial form of religion, the natural religion of reason that emerged during the Enlightenment.

The natural religion, then, is an extremely privatized religion that has been, as it were, specially prepared for the domestic use of the propertied middle-class citizen. It is above all a religion of inner feeling. It does not protest against or oppose in any way the definitions of reality, meaning or truth . . . that are accepted by the middle-class society of exchange and success [Metz 1980, 45].

Liberation theologians claim that abstract treatments of sin and redemption blind us to the concrete manifestations of sin, to the cultural structures of racism, sexism, and capitalism. Metz argues that concepts of sin and redemption which see sin as being in any way universally overcome in the life and death of Jesus are themselves masks for the continued existence of social structures of sinful exploitation and domination. He believes that Christianity cannot move beyond its oppressive function unless Christians forgo a transcendental understanding of their faith, a belief that the universal meaning of history and the historical identity of Christianity are already established, a belief that history has already been saved in the definitive eschatological action of God in Jesus Christ. Metz claims that universal Christianity legitimizes "the identity of the religious subject in view of the historical suffering of man [*sic*]" (Metz 1980, 45), for it assumes that Christian claims to redemption are somehow guaranteed. This idealistic approach amounts to a denial that Christian faith is always endangered. It is an evasion of what Metz identifies as "critical counterquestions":

> Where, for example, is the historical and social basis of the claim made by Christians to be the advocates of this universal and undivided justice? Where can concrete examples of the history of liberation be found in Christianity? . . . It is quite clear from these questions that the crisis in Christianity today is not primarily a crisis of the content of faith and its promises, but a crisis of subjects and institutions which do not measure up to the demands made by faith [Metz 1980, 45].

In contrast to the guaranteed victory over evil promised in Christian triumphalism, the claims of liberation theologians have a historical, concrete basis: the experience of redemption in base Christian communities, in the women's movement, in the black church. "Transcendence" is distinctly historical: it consists in the power to overcome given historical conditions. Transcendence is expressed as the freedom to resist and to overturn oppression. The power of community, of participation in a communal struggle for liberation, is also a form of transcendence. Soelle claims that the focus of a liberating Christianity is not life after death, but life *before* death. She states that the transcendence central to Christian faith lies not in the perfection of a God unfettered by history, but in the transpersonal power to resist given historical structures of domination (Soelle 1978, 34).

The collective struggle that continues beyond the efforts of an individual is also a form of transcendence. The concept of God is correlative with "this worldly transcendence." God is named as that which is in, enables, or grounds liberating communities. Miranda provides a similar reinterpretation of transcendence and a description of a freeing God:

> The God who does not allow himself [*sic*] to be objectified, because only in the immediate command of conscience is he [*sic*] God, clearly specifies that he [*sic*] is knowable exclusively in the cry of the poor and the weak who seek justice. . . . Transcendence does not mean only an

unimaginable and inconceivable God, but a God who is accessible only in the act of justice [Miranda 1974, 48].

Liberation and the Essence of Christianity

The sharp critiques and clear reformulations of traditional Christian doctrines found in liberation theology are all predicated upon a single base: the ultimate significance of resistance and liberation. Liberating communities of faith show no separation between the spiritual and the political. The worth of human life is undivided; spiritual transformation is inextricably tied to social and political transformation. These claims are radical; the practice they reflect and enhance is revolutionary.

These far-reaching reinterpretations of faith and theology pose disturbing questions for traditional theologians. If an interpretation of biblical traditions from the perspective of the marginal leads to drastically different readings of those texts, how does one adjudicate the truth-claims of different interpretations? Could it be possible that scholarly interpretations are not at all objective, but reflect the meaning of faith for those who are middle class, not the meaning of Christian faith for anyone in any other situation? If the politics of faith communities and the meaning of biblical traditions are so exclusively determined by the social and political location of those who read the texts, how are judgments of truth ever to be made?

Many theologians attempt to answer such questions by evaluating their own interpretations in light of the independent meaning of biblical traditions or in light of the essence of Christian faith. Soelle, for example, states that the essence of the gospel is the liberation of all: "It is concerned with the oppressed, the poor, those who mourn" (Soelle 1974, 67). James Cone makes an even stronger claim about the truth of black theology: "Any view of the gospel that fails to understand the Church as that community whose work and consciousness are defined by the community of the oppressed is not Christian and is thus heretical" (Cone 1975, 37).

It is at this point that I find myself unable to follow most liberation theologians. What is the meaning of truth in communities of liberation? Is the gospel true because it frees? Or do we know that the truth of faith is found in commitment to the oppressed because this is the "real" meaning of the gospel?

The two dimensions of my context—oppressed and oppressor—lead to two types of questions about the truth of Christian faith. First, as one who is oppressed because of my sex, I am critical of attempts to establish the truth of faith by showing its correspondence with what is universal about human being. I am increasingly aware that to speak of the universal is all too often, and perhaps even necessarily, to elevate as universal and normative a particular aspect of human being. Throughout this work I explore the dangers of appealing to universal categories and point to the many instances in which the features of existence predominant in the lives of white men are taken as universal and the experience of women and people of color is ignored.

Second, as an oppressor I am uncomfortable with another way of defining truth. I am not able to state that liberation theology and liberation faith are true because they are authentically Christian. As one who is both an oppressor and a Christian, I am painfully aware of the easy coexistence of Christianity and structures of oppression. While it may be valid for others in different contexts to ground the truth of their interpretation in the authority of the scriptural tradition, in my context such a construction of truth seems either naive or politically dangerous. For me to identify liberation theology as authentically Christian would be to evade the temporality of theological discourse. Such identification would diminish the complexity of the Christian tradition and attempt to elide the risks of the temporality of theological discourse by establishing a secure home for liberation theology within an ascertainable transcendent destiny or historical trajectory.

Within liberation theology and within my work as a feminist theologian of liberation, authentic Christianity is identified as that which liberates. The work of liberation theology is not without precedent; it is part of a revolutionary strand within the Christian tradition. Although this strand can easily be established as Christian—it relies on the Christian mythos and history for its interpretation of life in the present—there are dangers in a naive understanding of the import of that attribution for the establishment of the truth of liberation theology. I do not find it tenable to make its continuities with scripture and tradition the measure of the authenticity and truth of liberation faith. Even if one could establish that liberation faith is *continuous* with the Christian tradition, that would not establish its truth in a liberating way. Liberation faith could be continuous with a very persistent lie, a powerful system of oppression and ideological mystification. The identification of continuity with truth evades the complex historicity of discourse. It also evades the question of truth and attempts to return to a traditional notion of truth as propositional. In contrast, liberating faith attempts to posit a new criterion of truth: practice.

There are other reasons for avoiding a type of truth claim that equates continuity with truth. The revolutionary strand within the Christian tradition represents only one form of ecclesia, and a minority form at that. The dominant motifs within the history of the Christian tradition are more otherworldly and more accommodating to existing social structures. I am sensitive to this as a feminist, well aware that the Christian church has been a leading force in the suppression of women. I am also convinced by Marxist analyses of Christianity and histories, such as those of Paul Johnson, that demonstrate the ideological nature of Christian faith, its repeated support for hierarchical, elitist forms of government, and its opposition to social transformation (Johnson 1979).

My reservation in this case is based on my awareness of the paucity of a revolutionary form of Christian faith. Christianity has often been either repressive or quiescent. This historical predominance of other types of Christian faith raises difficulties in my mind about the claim to have found the authentic meaning of faith in work for liberation. For the claim to such an inheritance could be met equally well by alternate claims to correspondence to the scriptures, or to the teachings and practice of Jesus. The accommodationist can appeal to the otherwordly stratum in the gospels, to the antirevolutionary statements in scripture and in tradition. The precedents of revolutionary forms of ecclesia in the history of the church cannot match the precedents of a Christianity that has supported dominant cultural and governmental institutions. Christianity's history of cooperation with structures of domination extends from the time of Constantine to the conflation of God and patriotism in the United States.

The point of these caveats is not to deny the legitimacy of my and other liberation theologians' identifying ourselves as Christian but to point to the limited impact of this identification. The marks that we use to identify ourselves as Christian, our similarity to motifs, themes, and practices of the church in the past, can be matched and even surpassed by other, more conservative forms of Christianity. To argue that this one trajectory—liberation theology—represents the essence of Christianity would require warrants other than a claim of correspondence with a limited range of originating events. This claim is of limited value for two reasons. First, it is a claim that can be made with equal certainty by a plethora of positions. Second, it assumes that the truth of Christianity is somehow located in that which is most faithful to its origins, or in that which stays the same.

This second reason, dissatisfaction with equating truth with that which is original, lies in the disparity between that definition of truth and what I find to be the most exciting aspect of liberation faith, the verifying function of practice. I believe that Christianity contains something of truth not because of its origins, but because it liberates people now from specific forms of oppression. Similarly, the truth of liberation faith is rooted not so much in its correspondence with themes and practices of the church in the past, but in its power to liberate people in the present. This focus on truth being demonstrated in actual liberation is lost if one attempts to establish faith's authenticity on grounds of historical continuity.

All these difficulties can be summarized as follows. I bring two caveats against any claim that liberation theology or a feminist theology of liberation represents the essence of Christianity. The first caveat is based on the work of scholars like Käsemann and Pagels, which discloses the plurality of positions within even the earliest Christian communities. The origins and history of Christianity are complex and conflictual. It is not possible to sort out only one strand with a valid claim to unbroken continuity. There are many lines of continuity within the Christian tradition.

The second caveat is political. We must not evade pluralism; we must acknowledge the power, if not the singular authenticity, of many different trajectories within the Christian tradition. Differing interpretations of the nature of Christianity are not of mere intellectual interest, but have vital significance for the lives of many people. A triumphalistic interpretation of the nature of Christianity has resulted in heresy trials, anti-Semitism, the legitimation of empire, the murder of women accused of being witches. An otherworldly Christianity has sanctioned slavery, sexism, capitalism, racism, and the current rush toward nuclear holocaust.

It is, however, important to understand the relationship of liberating faith to Christian traditions. There are different options within the Christian tradition, and one of them is liberation theology. It is legitimate and honest for liberation theologians to point to their continuity with and rootedness in a particular history. The movement for liberation does not emerge in a vacuum, but is rooted in particular traditions and histories of resistance. To recover these histories is part of the task of maintaining dangerous memories.

The realm of the debate over the *truth* of various options should, however, be moved from a consideration of which trajectory is more continuous with the Christian past to a consideration of which is more liberating. This move entails two decisions. First, we must recognize that the essence of Christianity might in fact be oppressive rather than liberating. My task as a liberation theologian is to examine carefully the Christian tradition and be attentive to oppressive elements that continue in my own trajectory. This attention is required if I take seriously the oppressive impact of the Christian church throughout its history. It is naive to assume that this history represents a mere misinterpretation of Christian symbols. The question of how these symbols can be so easily misinterpreted in oppressive ways leads to the more radical question of whether the symbols themselves blind us to oppression.

Second, the epistemic shift constitutive of liberation theology must be taken seriously. The warrant for its validity is circular. Liberating faith begins with identification with the oppressed and justifies itself by whatever ends oppression. This is a dangerous, and to many, untenable position, a renunciation of the absoluteness of Christian faith.

I would recast liberation theology's claim to represent the essence of Christianity in this way: the content of liberation theology is the recovery of one stratum within the Christian tradition (a particular option that is critical of society and of the institutional church). Liberation theology is a practical, communal, revolutionary type of ecclesia that is rooted in the Christian past and worthy of further implementation in the present and future. Liberation theology presents one with the choice to be part of the underground church, part of the Christianity that has been committed to liberation in history and to solidarity with the oppressed.

4

Strategic Knowledges

In the preceding chapter I described the correspondence between the methods and presuppositions of liberation theology and the similar aims and warrants in Foucault's genealogy. Both forms of discourse disclose memories of conflict and recover suppressed knowledges. These tasks of disclosure and discovery may seem innocuous, a mere rediscovery of excluded knowledges. There is, however, another dimension to genealogy and to both liberation theology: the insurrection of subjugated knowledges. This third dimension changes the relative valence of theory and practice. Because of this shift, liberation theology is created primarily by activists, not scholars.

The third element of genealogy—the insurrection of subjugated knowledges—is the release of the memory of subjugation and the content of the knowledge that has been suppressed into struggle with dominant knowledges. Foucault describes the full task of genealogy as

> the attempt to emancipate historical knowledges from that subjection, to render them, that is, capable of opposition and of struggle against the coercion of a theoretical, unitary, formal and scientific discourse [Foucault 1980b, 85].

The first two elements of genealogy, the memory of conflict and the expression of alternate knowledges, are not complete without the third element: the struggle of those knowledges against dominant forms of discourse. It is in fulfilling this task that the strategic rather than the merely speculative nature of genealogical thought becomes apparent.

UNIVERSAL DISCOURSE AND THE ELISION OF OPPRESSION

The importance of strategy emerges from the tension inherent in the articulation of dangerous memories. This tension impels liberation thinkers toward action, toward the formation of political strategies, and away from primarily theoretical work. Feminist theologians, for example, criticize academic theologians and philosophers for their elision of the specificity of men's oppression of women. As Mary Daly so cogently argues, their tendency to speak of sin in abstract terms, their attempt to uncover what is universal about sin or about human evil, blinds them to even the most blatant forms of oppression and exclusion in their own social worlds.

> . . . the lack of explicit relevance of intellection to the fact of oppression in its precise forms, such as sexual hierarchy, is itself oppressive. This is the case when theologians write long treatises on creative hope, political theology, or revolution without any specific acknowledgment of or application to the problem of sexism or other specific forms of injustice. . . . Tillich's ontological theology, too, although it is potentially liberating in a very radical sense, fails to be adequate in this regard [Daly 1973, 20–21].

Daly claims that by speaking of sin in abstract universal categories, theologians such as Tillich have left unexamined the deadly pervasiveness of sexism in Western culture.

> Tillich has rightly shown that "all problems of love, power, and justice drive us to an ontological analysis." What his analysis leaves out is the essential fact that division by socialization into sex roles divides the human psyche itself, so that love cut off from power and justice is pseudo-love, power isolated from love and justice is inauthentic power of dominance, and justice is a meaningless facade of legalism split off from love and real power of being. Without a perception of the demonic divisiveness of sex role socialization an "ontological" analysis of these problems remains hopelessly sterile and removed from the concrete conditions of existence [Daly 1973, 127].

This critique is not an external one. It is possible that there is an inherent connection between the universalism of theology with its elision of specific forms of evil and the existence of structures within society and the church that devalue women of all races, men of color, nature, and the body. Institutional structures of exclusion are akin to traditional theology in their disdain for the concrete, in the diminution of the value of the historical and specific, in their emphasis on what is universal or enduring as the locus of truth and significance. It is more important for theologians to address the structures of human being that enable sin and redemption, structures that perdure, than to confront and disclose specific manifestations of sin such as racism and sexism.

The Discourse of Resistance

A theologian who works within the horizon of specific manifestations of sin, whether racism, sexism, or militarism, finds herself or himself reshaping the very categories of theological reflection. Turning to particular histories of oppression does not mean that traditional theology has discovered a new subject that can be examined with its usual tools of thought. The new subject—the particular histories of oppression—requires new tools, new ways of determining the range of thought and the criteria with which to work. Mary Daly, for example, claims that feminist theology breaks the bonds of existing disciplines, creating new forms of thought, new ways of speaking.

> It is this holistic process of knowing that can make Gyn/Ecology the O-ology of all the -ologies, encircling them, spinning around and through them, unmasking their emptiness. As the O-ology of all the -ologies, Gyn/Ecology can reduce their pretentious facades to Zero. It can free the flow of their "courses" and overcome their necrophilic circles, their self-enclosed processions, through spiraling creative process. It is women's own Gyn/Ecology that can break the brokenness of the "field," deriding their borders and boundaries, changing the nouns of knowledge into verbs of knowing [Daly 1978, 11].

A reconsideration of the categories of knowledge appropriate to liberating faith is very close to the strategic element of genealogical work. Both types of thought attempt to discover a mode of reflection that can not only discover and disclose apparatuses of oppression, but can also aid the process of revolt against that oppression. Daly's *Gyn/Ecology* is not merely the description of women's experience but is itself an important tool in freeing women to name their own experience and to shape their world. Foucault's histories have a similar influence; they are histories for the present, strategically important weapons in a struggle for power (Foucault 1979, 31). Foucault's histories examine the specificity of power relations: the exclusions, rarities, and affirmations constitutive of a particular form of discourse. They are descriptions of the constitution of certain discourses from the perspective of the excluded who are struggling against those apparatuses of power/knowledge.

A Strategic Aim

The aim of liberation theology, of a feminist theology of liberation, and of Foucault's work, is not scientific but strategic. That is, our aim is not the construction of a definitive theory of human nature, sociality, and historicity based on an analysis of particular expressions of power. Liberation theologians such as Gutiérrez claim that the prior task of theology is responsiveness to the needs of the oppressed.

> . . . liberation theology's first question cannot be the same one that progressivist theology has asked since Bonhoeffer. The question is not how we are to talk about God in a world come of age, but how we are to

tell people who are scarcely human that God is love and that God's love makes us one family. The interlocutors of liberation theology are the nonpersons, the humans who are not considered human by the dominant social order—the poor, the exploited classes, the marginalized races, all the despised cultures [Gutiérrez 1978, 241].

Liberation theology is done with a recognition that "the system that meant intellectual and political freedom and economic opportunity for Europe and the United States . . . brought only new forms of oppression and exploitation to the common people of Latin America" (Gutiérrez 1978, 237). Recognition of the imperative of addressing problems of human suffering and not just the intellectual problems of an elite also shapes the method of political theology. Metz is not alone in his call for a new type of thought, one that emerges from action in solidarity with all those who suffer.

Political consciousness *ex memoria passionis*, political action in the memory of mankind's [*sic*] history of suffering: this could indicate an understanding of politics that would lead to new possibilities and new criteria. . . . It offers inspiration for a new form of solidarity. . . . It excludes any form of freedom and peace at the expense of the suppressed history of suffering of other nations and groups [Metz 1980, 105].

Attentiveness to human suffering means that we theologians must increase our awareness of the different manifestations of human experience and confront the exploitative, oppressive underside of the Enlightenment, of Western rationality and Western humanism, the paternalism and oppression of Christian triumphalism. Following this line of reasoning has led Foucault to question the political integrity and intellectual honesty of the scientific method itself. He states that his work, insofar as it is genealogical, insofar as it is attentive to the voices of the excluded, is antiscientific. He argues not against rigorous thought per se, but against science as it specifically excludes certain knowers and types of knowledge (Foucault 1980b, 83–84). His concern is expressed in his objection to attempts to establish Marxism as a science.

What types of knowledge do you want to disqualify in the very instant of your demand: "Is it a science"? Which speaking, discoursing subjects—which subjects of experience and knowledge—do you then want to "diminish" when you say: "I who conduct this discourse am conducting a scientific discourse, and I am a scientist"? Which theoretical-political *avant garde* do you want to enthrone in order to isolate it from all the discontinuous forms of knowledge that circulate about it? [Foucault 1980b, 85].

Strategists of Life and Death

Why is there resistance to universalism and scientificity in Foucault, in liberation theology, and in a feminist theology of liberation? Why is it not ultimately trivial to focus exclusively on particular modifications of human being and social structures?

Foucault states that in our time the intellectual is "no longer the rhapsodist of the eternal, but the strategist of life and death" (Foucault 1980b, 129). Liberation theology and a feminist theology of liberation are also strategies of life and death. They result from the choice of a specific and timely focus. Liberation and feminist theologians have three basic reasons for opting for specificity, particularity, and strategy over more ontological and universal considerations. First, if we fail to give enough attention to the political and social history of Christianity, its practical impact (as well as its "eternal" or "universal" truths about human nature and human possibilities) will not be felt and the denial by the church and by Western culture of full humanity to women and minorities will be veiled.

A second reason for choosing strategic thought stems from the continued parochialism of supposedly universally valid systems. A definition of Christianity and of humanity based on the experience only of the dominant class has been misunderstood as universal. The experience of those who do not belong to the dominant class is regarded as only a modification of what is universal. The result is unabashed theological imperialism. The male experience of sin and redemption is identified as the human experience of sin and redemption; Western Christianity is exported to other nations and cultures as the definitive disclosure of the divine-human relationship.

A third reason for the specific focus of theologies of liberation is the need for attention to alternate visions of power, community, and faith present in formerly excluded groups. Daly finds in women's experience, for example, an acceptance of interdependence and mutuality that counters masculine individualism, a rootedness and acceptance of finitude, the transience of nature and the body, sharply divergent from a masculine emphasis on spirit, transcendence, identity, and permanence. She describes a diverse community of women:

> Haggard Journeyers move alone and together away from the Haunted Houses and Zoos that are filled with mirrors/mirages/manacles intended to hold us in captivity. "Together" does not mean in lockstep or simultaneously, but each according to her own Life-time. The moving presence of each Self calls forth the living presence of other journeying/enspiriting selves [Daly 1978, 366].

Women's "bonding" allows difference. Daly sharply contrasts this friendship with male bonding, a bonding that erases difference and denies change.

Such male merging in "the fire of communal ecstasy" or as "cells in a military organism" is necrophilic self-loss. In contrast to this, the Fire of Sisterhood results from the Sparking of Female Selves who are finding each other. It is the unleashing of biophilic energy. Furies spark new ideas, new words, new images, new feelings, new life, New Be-ing. . . . Since Sisterhood is the expression of biophilic energy burning through the encasements of the Necrophilic State of Staledom, it is more complex than mere male monogender merging [Daly 1978, 370].

Visions of human community different from those of modern patriarchal and technological society are shared among women of all races and by people of color. In the Native American traditions, for example, we find an alternate worldview expressed in their attitude toward nature. Nature is permeated by the sacred and humanity, far from being above nature, has value only within nature. This worldview counters the Western subordination of nature to humanity, a worldview that legitimates the devastation and exploitation of the earth.

Every part of this soil is sacred to my people. Every hillside, every valley, every plain and grove has been hallowed by some sad or happy event in days long vanished. The very dust upon which you now stand responds more lovingly to our footsteps than to yours, because it is rich with the blood of our ancestors, and our bare feet are conscious of the sympathetic touch.[1]

These alternative visions are not frivolous. They are serious alternatives to a culture that is quantitatively and qualitatively deadly. The implementation, and not just the discovery, of these visions is crucial because of the genocidal possibilities of modern cultures. The work of liberation theologians and feminist theologians of liberation addresses issues that are "ultimate," but not in a universal or eternal sense. We examine specific histories of oppression and point to the consequences of oppression. Sexism and racism, for example, have caused the distortion of the humanity of millions of people. Liberation theologians speak of the memory of all those who are denied access to education, to work, to independence, and to participation in the formation of culture and society on the bases of their sex and race. The exclusion of the poor from the center of attention has led to the death of millions through starvation; they are victims of an inequitable economic system.

The exclusion of the oppressed has far-reaching consequences. Qualitatively, Western culture seems to be moving toward the elimination of what has been regarded as the essence of human being—human dignity, freedom in decision making, participation in political and moral choices—through the mechanization and technological determination of human being and society. In work, in politics, choices are made by experts who are guided not by moral values but by the functional demands of efficiency and survival. Jürgen Habermas cites Luhmann's planning theory as an example. The need for planning theory is grounded in the problem of world complexity:

> Luhmann's planning theory marks out one of these types of politics as appropriate for complex societies, namely, comprehensive, non-participatory planning . . . the reproduction of highly complex societies leaves no choice but that of anchoring the required reflexivity of society in an administrative system shielded from the parties and the public, instead of in a democratically organized public domain [Habermas 1973, 134].

The human species is also threatened by extinction through nuclear holocaust and ecological disasters; both phenomena are not abberations but are rooted in particular understandings of power and of the relationship between nature and humanity. Their root lies in the Western idea of the transcendence of humanity over nature, in a concept of power as the ability to control and dominate. Intellectuals concerned with liberation turn to specific critiques of these manifestations of power because our time is one of unprecedented crisis: there are immediate threats to the lives of women, to the poor, to those oppressed in Central America, to the continued existence of the human species.

POWER AND IDEOLOGY

Many liberation theologians use a Marxist critique of ideology in their attempts to disclose and challenge oppressive theological concepts and church structures, exploitative social and political institutions. To state that ideas or institutions are ideological is to say that they mask relations of domination. Concern with such masking is obviously imperative in Foucault's genealogies. Part of the method of genealogy is, therefore, similar to ideology critique. In both, memories of suppressed conflicts are released, thereby exposing hidden power conflicts. Although these forms of critique are superficially similar, there are important differences between them. Ideology critique and its correlative discipline, the sociology of knowledge, examine only the conditions of knowledge and the distortions of that knowledge. Interrogation that uses these methods does not lead to a reconceptualization of the nature of knowledge itself. Ideology critique and the sociology of knowledge do not bring us to the epistemological level operative in Foucault's recasting of power/knowledge as one word. To work within the categories of a critique of ideology and a sociology of knowledge is to examine power and knowledge as two variables, ascertaining the particular modifications each induces from the other.

Genealogy brings forth a more subtle and more variegated understanding of power than does ideology critique. The categories of ideology critique are useful primarily in identifying the influence of class interests on the history of ideas. Foucault leads us to a wider notion of power. The power that influences ideas is not merely one of class interests, and the range of influence is much greater than the distortion of systems of thought. Power is multifarious, influencing what may count as true. It reflects the interests of many groups, and its influence goes beyond mere distortion. The salient characteristic of power in our time, for example, is its role in the production of life. Foucault's broader understanding of power as something that affects all aspects of life is based on our times' technology of power.

> The disciplines of the body and the regulations of the population constituted the two poles around which the organization of power over life was deployed. The setting up, in the course of the classical age, of this great bipolar technology—anatomic and biological, individualizing and specifying, directed toward the performances of the body, with attention to the processes of life—characterized a power whose highest function was perhaps no longer to kill, but to invest life through and through [Foucault 1980a, 139].

This era of "biopower" has brought about the "entry of life into history, . . . the entry of phenomena peculiar to the life of the human species into the order of knowledge and power, into the sphere of political techniques" (Foucault 1980a, 141–142). The development of educational institutions (universities, public schools), population control, and public-health measures marks the entry of the fact of living "into knowledge's field of control and power's sphere of intervention" (Foucault 1980a, 142, 140).

Genealogy is critical of all these technologies of power; its point of reference and of criticism is not merely the class interests of the proletariat. The location of critique in the class interests of the proletariat is seen by Foucault as inadequate for two reasons. First, critique based on the universal interests of the species as manifest in a particular class tends toward abstraction. Foucault criticizes the notion that the proletariat is the unconscious bearer of universal values and the intellectual is the spokesperson for the proletariat (Foucault 1980b, 126). The centrality of an intellectual avant-garde makes absolute what is only a particular perspective, thus excluding other perspectives and mystifying the power relationships inherent in any identification of particular knowers with the universally human.

Second, Foucault questions the actuality of the proletariat. Instead of reifying a particular class, Foucault points to subtle and variegated forms of resistance as the locus of critique, arguing that one can identify only a proletarian quality, a tendency toward resistance, not ubiquitous bearers of a uniform style of resistance to domination (Foucault 1980b, 137–138).

Foucault further criticizes ideology critique in that it tends to simplistically correlate power and falsity, arguing that determination by interests or by power relations inevitably distorts knowledge. Thus, to correlate a system of knowledge with power relations is to invalidate it, to demonstrate that it is not true. Foucault identifies this tendency as a nostalgia for simple, pure truth, a longing for absolute truth, truth untouched by the contingency and sociality of human knowing (Foucault 1980b, 118).

Foucault criticizes relations of power, just as ideology critique does, but not because they distort our understanding of something that is true; for example, the nature of human society or the possible distribution of wealth. His criticism is more complex. Foucault criticizes not a distortion of a primary truth but the production of particular truths. Power is not merely mystifying or distorting. Its most dangerous impact is its positive relation to truth, the effects of truth that it produces.

> I have been trying to make visible the constant articulation I think there is of power on knowledge and of knowledge on power. We should not be content to say that power has a need for such and such a discovery, such and such a form of knowledge, but we should add that the exercise of power itself creates and causes to emerge new objects of knowledge and accumulates new bodies of information. One can understand nothing about economic science if one does not know how power and economic power are exercised in everyday life. The exercise of power perpetually creates knowledge and, conversely, knowledge constantly induces effects of power [Foucault 1980b, 51–52].

Foucault's critiques exemplify his complex understanding of power. He does not criticize penology, for example, merely because class interests led to a distortion in our understanding of the nature of criminality. He holds up for description, analysis, and critique penology's effects of truth, the constitution of a delinquent population. Penology is ideological; it does reflect class interests. But penology is much more than a mere distortion. It led to the creation of something real, a delinquent population. Thus the "effects of truth" of penology, the changes it created in social and political life, are more important than its ideological falsity. One interpreter of Foucault, Colin Gordon, describes this nonideological aspect of power as follows:

> . . . if certain knowledges of "Man" are able to serve a technological function in the domination of people, this is not so much thanks to their capacity to establish a reign of ideological mystification as to their ability to define a certain field of empirical truth [Gordon 1980, 237].

Foucault thus teaches us that the productive aspects of power are more dangerous than the mystifying or falsifying ones. With such an emphasis, Foucault names clearly what is operative in many forms of liberation theology—a critique of the "positive" effects, and not merely the distortions, of theological symbols and doctrines. As a feminist theologian, I criticize the patriarchal concept of God not because it falsifies the essence of deity but because of its effects of truth, the type of human subjectivity and society that it produces: the domination of women by men and the self-deprecation of women. My critique focuses on the particular result of a given apparatus of power/knowledge and not the relation of power/knowledge per se.

THE POLITICS OF LIBERATION THEOLOGY

One of the most frequently stated claims of liberation theology is that theology should be done from the perspective of the oppressed. In this location with the oppressed, the intrinsically strategic nature of liberation theology is acknowledged. According to John Shelley, liberation theologians argue that all thought is intrinsically political, that it represents the perspective of one side or another in a struggle that is ongoing in our society, and that to deny that one-sidedness or to attempt to transcend that particularity is only to mystify it.

> But there is no pure ecclesiastical neutrality, just as there is no apolitical theology; there are only those who are conscious of their political assumptions and consequences and those who are not. Hence it is not a matter of purifying theology and the church of all social and political implications, but of bringing such implications to the attention of theology and encouraging it to reflect critically and responsibly on them [Shelley 1974, xiv].

Liberation theologians such as Robert McAfee Brown explicitly acknowledge their role in political struggles.

> Concern for liberation does not arise from theologians looking for new intellectual toys; it arises from the reality of grinding poverty, the distended stomachs of starving children, the brutality of political repression, and from a recognition that the Christian gospel announces the possibility of liberation from just such evils [Brown 1976, xv].

The theological work that responds to political concerns is strategic rather than speculative. Liberation theologians do not analyze the nature of love in itself, but examine concrete social conditions that subvert the possibility of love being expressed. Soelle, for example, speaks of the impossibility of fulfilling the imperative of love when economic conditions require working in a factory that produces napalm. To preach the gospel of love requires challenging the economic conditions that subvert its expression.

> The statement "you shall be my people" becomes true if it affects the consumers, manufacturers, and salesmen of napalm; if, therefore, it opens men's [*sic*] eyes to their role in destroying the very life that was promised to all men [*sic*] together [Soelle 1974, 77].

Feminist analyses of the pervasiveness of sexism point to the near impossibility of mutuality and love between men and women, an impossibility engendered by the "state of war" between men and women in patriarchal societies.

Even novice Furies are accused of thinking or saying that "men are the enemy." This is a subtly deceptive reversal, implying that women are the initiators of enmity, blaming the victims for The War. Its deceptive power is derived from the fact that the Fury in every woman does fight back against males and male institutions that target her as The Enemy. The point is that she did not create The War, but rather finds herself in a set-up in which fighting is necessary for Surviving. An obvious consequence of this situation is the fact that patriarchal males are the enemies of women. However, the fighter role of Furies is a derivative status, necessitated by the fact that women are the primal objects of patriarchal attack [Daly 1978, 364–365].

In each of these cases, the concern of theologians is with political struggles. To be true to this concern is to speak for particular human rights, not for universal human rights. To be a theologian of liberation is to be engaged in specific battles for justice, to work for social structures that enable, rather than destroy, possibilities for justice and human dignity. In such struggles, the work of the intellectual is not primarily to articulate the imperative of human dignity or justice from a universal base, say, natural law. The intellectual's work is more specific, since the challenge is to establish just conditions in reality.

Participating with the oppressed in struggles for justice changes the contours of the theoretician's work. Instead of merely articulating the demand for justice, the theoretician analyzes the concrete conditions that deny justice. The necessity for this type of investigation seems obvious. However, too often an abstract argument for justice is put forth, and unless it is accompanied by attention to the specific conditions that deny justice, change does not occur. It is easy to state that all races are equal; it is more difficult to ferret out the manifestations of racism that prevent the actualization of this ideal.

Liberation theologians are right to point out the result of the Christian tradition's abstract focus on ideals. By speaking of universals—of universal human rights, of universal peace—the Christian tradition fails to address concretely the specific threats to those rights and to peace, such as the alienation caused by capitalism and the threat of nuclear war.

By operating from the perspective of the oppressed, liberation theologians claim that the nature of Christian faith is intrinsically political, that it places one in a struggle for specific social conditions, that it is relevant not primarily in terms of universals but in terms of particulars: it is directed not toward the human in itself but toward the human as sinner. A liberating Christian faith addresses conditions of fallenness with a hope and a struggle for redemption. It is an intrinsically historical faith directed toward the denunciation and transformation of specific forms of oppression.

In the articulation of a critique of traditional theology and in an expression of alternate understandings of faith, liberation theologians and feminist theologians of liberation move toward a type of thought in which anthropology is not foundational. Although this is not thematized by other liberation theologians, I find that their vision is not based on anthropology but emerges from communal struggles for a particular kind of humanity. This particularity and communality are important aspects of an identification with the oppressed. In this identification we find a particularity that moves theology beyond idealistic attempts to ground social critique in anthropology.

This move occurs in two ways. First, the type of humanity envisioned by liberation theologians does not come about naturally; it has to be achieved. This type of human community is not a given; it must be fought for. Even then, it can be, and often is, destroyed in history. It is to be achieved, not merely recognized. Liberation theology is part of a struggle for the establishment of a particular kind of subjectivity, not a declaration of the a priori existence of that subjectivity.

In such work, concepts of faith and of God are correspondingly relativized. The foundation of liberation theology is a particular history and a particular God. Metz describes liberation theology emerging from commitment to processes in history in which community is created, in which people are freed.

> The universality of the offer of salvation in Christianity does not have the character of a transcendental or universally historical concept of universality. It has rather the character of an "invitation." The inviting logos of Christianity does not in any sense compel. It has a narrative structure with a practical and liberating intention. If this is expressed in Christological terms, it means that the salvation that is founded "for all men" [sic] in Christ does not become universal via an idea, but via the intelligible power of a praxis, the praxis of following Christ [Metz 1980, 165].

There is a second way in which liberation theology's critical thought moves beyond idealistic attempts to ground social critique in anthropology. This critique emerges from within the struggle for liberation. It is not the result of speculation divorced from revolutionary practice. The faith stance of liberation theology, the claim that it is possible to construct a society based on solidarity, seems at first glance impossible and not significantly different from the unattainable monotheistic ideal criticized by Steiner (1971, 44–45). It is important, therefore, to turn again to the perspective of the oppressed as the basis of liberation theology's vision. The claim that solidarity and justice are impossible arises when those ideals are posed conceptually or abstractly—

as achieved already in the life of Jesus, as givens—and not rooted in a particular form of ecclesia. The ideals of a liberating faith are not duties or imperatives; they emerge naturally from identification with the oppressed, from the experience of community with the oppressed. The power of relatedness in ecclesia does not demand love and solidarity but enables and evokes it.

The symbolic language of grace is appropriate at this point: the ability to love and to work for justice is something we are given through the power of community. An attempt to bring justice does not make sense as an abstract imperative or judgment outside of this communal context. Within a liberating faith we find social structures that mediate the divine and enable solidarity, rather than an abstract call to justice. The imperative of justice is motivated not by guilt or duty, but by love, by the power of relatedness.

A GENEALOGY OF OPPRESSION

Thus far I have argued that liberation thought reflects more the challenge of the specific than the universal intellectual. It is similar to Foucault's genealogical task in all its dimensions: the recovery of memories of conflict and exclusion, the disclosure of subjugated knowledges, and the bringing of these knowledges into play in political struggles.

An understanding of the genealogical method would be best gained, of course, by examining a complete genealogy. Here I will only indicate the contours of a complete genealogy by summarizing Foucault's contrast of a genealogical and a historical interrogation of a specific form of oppression: the imprisonment of political dissidents in the Soviet Union, the system known as the Gulag.

Theoretical Reduction

Foucault first challenges the theoretical reduction of the Gulag question: the attempt to understand the Gulag system as an error, a betrayal of the theory of Marx and Lenin (Foucault 1980b, 137). This reduction is described as

> refusing to question the Gulag on the basis of the texts of Marx or Lenin or to ask oneself how, through what error, deviation, misunderstanding or distortion of speculation or practice, their theory could have been betrayed to such a degree. On the contrary, it means questioning all those theoretical texts, however old, from the standpoint of the reality of the Gulag. Rather than of searching in those texts for a condemnation in advance of the Gulag, it is a matter of asking what in those texts could have made the Gulag possible, what might even now continue to justify it, and what makes its intolerable truths still accepted today. The Gulag question must not be posed in terms of error (reduction of the problem to one of theory) but in terms of reality [Foucault 1980b, 135].

The shift in questioning is from theory to practice. The Gulag is not understood merely as a theoretical problem, a matter of correct interpretation and application. This type of questioning also characterizes feminist theology. Instead of asking about ideological distortions or misuse of Christian symbols and concepts, radical feminist theologians examine the ideological *nature* of the Christian faith and its symbols, asking what it is about Christian faith itself that makes the oppression of women actual in history. Mary Daly, for example, claims that myths "stage" reality. The patriarchal influence of the Christian church in society is not a misinterpretation or distortion but constitutes the very substance of the Christian tradition. According to Daly, Christian myths and symbols program sexism and necrophilia:

> Western society is still possessed overtly and subliminally by Christian symbolism. . . . Its ultimate symbol of processions is the all-male trinity itself. . . . This mythic paradigm of the trinity is the product of Christian culture, but it is expressive of *all* patriarchal patterning of society. . . . Human males are eternally putting on the masks and playing the roles of the Divine Persons. The mundane processions of sons have as their basic but unacknowledged and unattainable aim an attempted "consubstantiality" with the father (the cosmic father, the oedipal father, the professional godfather). . . . Spirited by all these relations is the asphyxiating atmosphere of male bonding. And, as Virginia Woolf saw, the death-oriented military processions display the real direction of the whole scenario, which is a funeral procession engulfing all life forms. God the father requires total sacrifice/ destruction [Daly 1978, 45, 38–39].

Instead of finding what it is in Christian texts that condemns sexism in advance, radical feminists question the texts from the standpoint of sexism, asking what it is about Christian concepts of God, of history, and of human nature that made it possible for sexism to operate in the life of the Christian community. We find oppression at the heart of the Christian tradition: in the exclusively masculine symbolism for the divine; in a dualism that devalues the body and the historical; in a hierarchical understanding of power and the order of creation; in an imperial concept of divine power; in a triumphant, absolute christology; in definitions of sin as pride and rebellion—definitions that prevent revolt (Ruether 1975, 83). Like Foucault, some feminist theologians refuse to accept the theoretical reduction of the problem of sexism but examine what it is in the Christian tradition itself that justifies and perpetuates sexism.

Historicist Reduction

Foucault's genealogy also avoids a historicist reduction of the problem, making the Gulag an effect which can be sufficiently understood by finding its causes (Foucault 1980b, 137). With this demurral, we move to an alternate type of investigation with wide implications for liberation theology. Foucault argues that one must not

> . . . restrict one's questioning to the level of cause. If one begins by asking for the "cause" of the Gulag (Russia's retarded development, the transformation of the party into a bureaucracy, the specific economic difficulties of the USSR), one makes the Gulag appear as a sort of disease or abscess, an infection, degeneration or involution. This is to think of the Gulag only negatively, as an obstacle to be removed. . . . The Gulag question has to be posed in positive terms. The problem of causes must not be dissociated from that of function: what use is the Gulag, what functions does it assure, in what strategies is it integrated? [Foucault 1980b, 135–136].

Following this line of argument would dispel any tendencies to focus on merely ideological uses or distortions of the Christian tradition. A historicist reduction would explain the oppressive impact of the Christian tradition in terms of such causes as the patriarchal culture in which the first Christian communities emerged, a cultural milieu which necessitated masculine language for deity and the leadership of men within the church; the lack of sufficient influence for political change, thus the individualistic or otherworldly interpretation of the Christian ethos. Other historical causes given for the oppressive aspects of the Christian tradition might be the imperatives of survival and the need for hierarchical institutionalization or accommodation to insure the continuance of the tradition. Although such causes may be operative, this type of analysis becomes reductionist if the positive functions of the oppressive aspects of the tradition are not addressed.

Feminist theology examines the oppressive aspects of the Christian tradition, its masculine language for God, its dualism, and its denigration of women as weak and responsible for sin in terms of their function within Christianity. Feminist theologians examine the type of human community these "distortions" evoke and sustain. From this perspective, the predominance of masculine language for God is understood not merely in terms of an inevitable occurrence given the patriarchal culture within which Christianity first emerged, but in terms of the function of that language in reinforcing the domination of women by men.

> The biblical and popular image of God as a great patriarch in heaven, rewarding and punishing according to his mysterious and seemingly arbitrary will, has dominated the imagination of millions over thousands of years. The symbol of the Father God, spawned in the human imagination and sustained as plausible by patriarchy, has in turn rendered service to this type of society by making its mechanisms

for the oppression of women appear right and fitting. If God in "his" heaven is a father ruling "his" people, then it is in the "nature" of things and according to divine plan and the order of the universe that society be male-dominated [Daly 1973, 13].

A radical feminist critique avoids a historicist reduction of the problem of sexism and instead examines the function of sexism in the Christian tradition. Sexism is not only a distortion of the Christian tradition; it also provides security in the face of contingency and dependence. Mary Daly writes that in sexism and its devaluation of the feminine, the historical, and the contingent, we find a fundamental refusal of finitude and an attempt to overcome the limits of human existence (Daly 1978, 37–112). An imperialist and sexist concept of God is not merely an ideological distortion of the Christian revelation of God; it serves to remove some of the risk of belonging to history. The concept of an individual's relation with God as primarily subjective and individualistic is not merely ideological; it has the function of removing people from the bloody arena of historical struggle and responsibility. The concept of an omnipotent providential deity serves to subvert rebellion and remove the imperative of responsibility for social change: This function is not only ideological, masking the nonnecessity of conditions that are oppressive; it also insures or enhances the survival of a social system by eliciting accommodation to it.

The power and persistence of repressive aspects of the Christian tradition cannot be understood if they are approached only as ideological distortions. The history of Christianity's complicity with oppressive and authoritarian governments, from Constantine through the Crusades to the silence of much of the German church regarding Hitler, is not understood when oppressive practices are viewed as distortions. The function of these "distortions" within the Christian tradition and within the wider social system must be addressed.

Utopian Dissolution

Foucault's genealogy also rejects "a utopian dissolution" of the Gulag problem, a critique of an oppressive practice by contrasting it with an ideal standard (Foucault 1980b, 137). He states that we must refuse

> . . . to adopt for the critique of the Gulag a law or principle of selection internal to our own discourse or dream. By this I mean . . . not attempting to evade the problem by putting inverted commas . . . around Soviet socialism in order to protect the good, true socialism, . . . which alone can provide a legitimate standpoint for a politically valid critique. . . . We must open our eyes on the contrary to what enables people there . . . to resist the Gulag, what makes it intolerable for them, and what can give the people of that anti-Gulag the courage to stand up and

die in order to be able to utter a word or a poem. . . . We should listen
to these people, not to our century-old little love song for "socialism."
. . . The leverage against the Gulag is not in our heads, but in their
bodies, their energy, what they say, think and do [Foucault 1980b, 136].

Foucault challenges us to recognize the folly of criticizing oppression in
terms of the "real Christianity." The basis of critique is not abstract ideas,
but women and men who challenge oppressive institutions. We theologians
of liberation should listen to what it is that makes it possible for people to
resist. Liberation theology does not so much evoke a faith that leads to resistance as it reflects on the lives of women and men devoted to freedom and
justice.

Universalizing Dissolution

A fourth evasion is described by Foucault: "a universalizing dissolution"
of the problem, an examination of the general problem of internment rather
than the role of the Gulag within socialism (Foucault 1980b, 137).

The Gulag is not a question to be posed for any and every country. It
has to be posed for every *socialist* country, insofar as none of these since
1917 has managed to function without a more-or-less developed Gulag
system [Foucault 1980b, 136–137].

Foucault again turns to the function of oppression, not allowing us the comfort of understanding oppression as accidental. Daly resists the same attempt
in theology. She argues that to focus on the problem of *human* oppression
and liberation, or sinfulness per se, is to avoid the question of the function of
sexism within the institutional structure of the Christian tradition, of the
pervasiveness of oppression within Christianity, of the perpetual denigration
of women by this specific tradition. It is not enough to analyze the problems
of liberation and oppression; we must also understand the specific mechanisms of oppression and the functional aspects of that oppression that serve
to perpetuate it (Daly 1973, 20–21).

The specificity of genealogy precludes the conclusion that oppression is
merely epiphenomenal. The aim of genealogy is to understand the precise
mechanisms and functions of particular oppressions. This questioning is far-
reaching, leading to an examination of conventional structures of knowing
and valuing, and their relation to apparatuses of domination.

These concerns are not foreign to liberation theology. How do we begin to
understand the repeated complicity of the Christian church with sexism, with
racism, with economic exploitation? In my examination of this question, I
have repeatedly encountered problems caused by a turn to universals as the
measure of truth. One problem is a universalizing dissolution of the problem
of oppression, an examination of sin as a dimension of all human existence

rather than a challenge to the racism and sexism of the Christian tradition.

A too quick turn to universals hampers resistance. The women's movement, for example, is slowly learning to specify the nature of sexism, and does not take as definitive the experience of white middle-class women. The means by which white middle-class women resist are not always appropriate for women of other races and classes, whose resistance to sexism is more inextricably bound to struggles against economic exploitation. Middle-class women's demands for the opportunity to work and for equal rights do not encompass the demands of other women for jobs with dignity and fair wages, support for single-mother families, and freedom from discrimination on the basis of sexual preference.

I have repeatedly found distortions in attempts to produce a universally valid political or theoretical analysis. This leads me to question the principles of political and theoretical analysis, especially the definition of truth. Is a program for political action against patriarchy true if it can be employed by women in any culture, of any race? Are our visions of human community true if they represent the fulfillment of what is essential about all human beings?

I think that the answer to both these questions is no. The ideal of universal or absolute truth is intrinsically correlated with oppression. I find an openness to many different understandings of truth in the women's movement and in some segments of the peace movement. In sisterhood there is freedom from a self-securing that requires absolutizing one's perspective. In the Christian tradition, however, I find a pathological obsession with security, an obsession that impels the denial of difference (thus concern with heresy and essences), an obsession that leads to a blinding Christian triumphalism, an obsession that receives symbolic expression in the concept of the sovereignty of God.

In the next chapter I will explore an alternate "obsession," a commitment to relativism and to practice. The discussion of different methods of attaining truth may appear dangerously abstract. Although it is not as concrete as a genealogy of some specific apparatus of power/knowledge, this work in method is strategic. It is based in political activity and drives me to further political activity.

I could not ask these questions if I were not part of the women's movement, participating in and being challenged by efforts to rename and transform the world. I find in the women's movement acceptance of the new, the unique, the nonuniversal. I find in sisterhood a commitment to liberation and an openness to different ways of understanding and reaching liberation. Daly describes this openness as follows:

Recognizing the chasms of difference among sister voyagers is coming to understand the terrifying terrain through which we must travel together and apart. At the same time, the spaces between us are encouraging signs of our immeasurable unique potentialities. . . . The greatness of our differences signals the immensity/intensity of the Fire that will flame from our combined creative Fury [Daly 1978, 382].

The value of an alternate approach to difference, a method in attaining a truth that is diverse, changing, and political, is itself thoroughly strategic. This method leads to political activism, and its realm of verification is the political battle for truth.

5

The Truth of Liberation Theology: "Particulars of a Relative Sublime"

A feminist theology of liberation is part of an epistemic shift, a redefinition of the truth of Christian faith. The truth of Christian faith is at stake not in terms of its coherence with ontological structures and their potential modification, but in life and death struggles, in daily operations of power/knowledge. It is in this arena of the determination of the character of daily life that the truth of Christian faith, both its method and referent, must be determined. The battle against nihilism and oppression is not primarily conceptual but practical. The focus therefore of a liberating faith and of theology is not primarily the analysis of human being and its possibilities, but the creation of redeemed communities.

My feminist theology of liberation emerges from the tension I experience between skepticism and resistance to oppression and domination. The skeptical moment is rooted in my awareness of the power and peril of discourse, my encounter with the transitory nature of "the order of things," and my acknowledgment of the effects of truth resident within forms of discourse, the continued operation of power as intrinsic to all discourse, including my own.

Entanglement in power and particularity is not a condition to be avoided, but one to be understood. This becomes ironically clear as I realize that the very possibility of critique and of resistance is rooted not in a universal sense of justice, but in concrete, varied, tenuous experiences of resistance and liberation, that is, in my participation in different forms of power/knowledge.

The seemingly positivistic work of genealogy—the critique of apparatuses of power/knowledge—occurs within a non-positivistic framework. Such a critique is possible because of a prior commitment to the oppressed, a prior belonging to another apparatus. Even in critique, then, the task of genealogy is constructive, for the critique of dominant systems and the disclosure of suppressed systems is part of an insurrection of subjugated knowledges.

In this work there is the disclosure of what might be called "proleptic universals," alternate visions of society, humanity, institutional structures, orders of knowing, that are then brought into play. While it may be unsettling to think only within these categories, it is not an endeavor without precedents. Richard Rorty describes this concept of truth in *Philosophy and the Mirror of Nature*. Rorty argues that it is possible to think if the claim to know essences is relinquished. He describes the philosophers who have made such claims.

> These peripheral, pragmatic philosophers are skeptical primarily *about systematic philosophy*, about the whole project of universal commensuration. . . . They (Heidegger, Wittgenstein, Dewey) hammer away at the holistic point that words take their meanings from other words rather than by virtue of their representative character, and the corollary that vocabularies acquire their privileges from the men [*sic*] who use them rather than from their transparency to the real [Rorty 1980, 368].

The wisdom found in these philosophers is a wisdom of conversation, an offering of another set of descriptive vocabularies without making the arrogant claim of disclosing the definitive commensurating vocabulary. Rorty finds this wisdom in the work of the edifying, as distinct from the systematic, philosophers.

> Edifying philosophers want to keep space open for that sense of wonder which poets can sometimes cause—wonder that there is something new under the sun, something which is *not* an accurate representation of what was already there, something which (at least for the moment) cannot be explained and can barely be described [Rorty 1980, 370].

THE PRIMACY OF THE PARTICULAR

Wallace Stevens is another writer whose thought avoids universals, and names, rather, the particular *as* particular.[1] In his poem "On the Road Home" he expresses the plenitude of particularity and the wealth of insight possible as one forgoes the search for absolutes and accepts and acknowledges the particular as such.

> It was when I said,
> "There is no such thing as the truth,"
> That the grapes seemed fatter.
> The fox ran out of his hole.

> You . . . You said,
> "There are many truths,
> But they are not parts of a truth."
> Then the tree, at night, began to change,
> smoking through green and smoking blue.

We were two figures in a wood.
We said we stood alone.

It was when I said,
"Words are not forms of a single word.
In the sum of the parts, there are only the parts.
The world must be measured by eye";

It was when you said, "the idols have seen lots of poverty,
Snakes and gold and lice,
But not the truth";

It was at that time, that the silence was largest
And longest, the night was roundest,
The fragrance of the autumn warmest,
Closest and strongest [Stevens 1972, 164–165].

I do not wish to leave a false impression by quoting this piece. Despite the lyrical quality of Stevens's poetry, it is not easy to maintain this mode of thought. Rorty claims that it can be maintained, that more traditional philosophers should avoid the "bad taste" of asking edifying philosophers to be ontological or systematic (Rorty 1980, 372). Rorty's gentility is misleading. A Foucaultian perspective lays bare the agony of this refusal. It is not easy to avoid the solace of universals. This is done only at great cost. To remain "edifying," to use Rorty's deceptively benign phrase, is a great risk.

Wallace Stevens expresses the pain as well as the promise of this choice. It does not always result in an experience of the plenitude of particularity. In "Chaos in Motion and Not in Motion" he speaks of the possible loss of all meaning following this refusal.

Oh, that this lashing wind was something more
Than the spirit of Ludwig Richter . . .
. . . .
People fall out of windows, trees tumble down,
Summer is changed to winter, the young grow old,

The air is full of children, statues, roofs
And snow. The theatre is spinning around,

Colliding with deaf-mute churches and optical trains.
The most massive sopranos are singing songs of scales.

And Ludwig Richter, turbulent Schlemihl,
Has lost the whole in which he was contained,

Knows desire without an object of desire,
All mind and violence and nothing felt.

He knows he has nothing more to think about,
Like the wind that lashes everything at once [Stevens 1972, 278].

The risk of chaos outside the safe boundaries of systematic, conventional thought is like the "earthquake phenomenon" described by Mary Daly, the loss of meaning that occurs in the process of creating meanings outside of patriarchy.

> Crones spinning closer and closer to the Center of our Centering Selves sometimes speak to each other of a certain experience which I shall call "the earthquake phenomenon." . . . A Crone may be moving swiftly over some ground and find/feel to her horror that it gapes open before her; there is a chasm at her feet. She must focus very quickly in order to strike a new balance. She holds fast until the horror passes, converting the necessary efforts of resistance into increasing assertion of her energy and discovery of latent power [Daly 1978, 409–410].

Daly finds it possible to affirm the particular after the earthquake. This affirmation is not so unequivocal in Stevens. Some of his later poetry has a tone of self-loathing and is suspicious of the disavowal of the absolute (see Stevens 1972, 240).

A resolutely particularistic style of thought does not represent merely the effort of brash minds to uncover the truth unencumbered by the weight of tradition. The passages from Daly and Stevens remind us that to reject the past and its forms of knowledge, to refuse to be at home in them any longer, is not a carefree attempt to live *de novo*. It is a painful refusal of what has been experienced as false security. This refusal is necessitated by an awareness that my work may well be, to quote Wallace Stevens, "disillusion as the last illusion."[2]

Strategic versus Theoretical Critique

The costliness of the endeavor to choose strategic over theoretical critique must be recognized in order to understand two things: the constant tendency to elide the reality of discourse and the importance of the refusal of that elision. I find it difficult to avoid returning to a former episteme in which faith means some sort of certainty. There are times when I return to absolutes. Yet I still maintain that for Christianity to remain critical, it must retain a skeptical edge. Without this edge, Christianity becomes oppressive. Without it, Christian affirmations lose their reference to concrete situations, a reference that arises from a self-conscious recognition of the inextricable fusion of power/knowledge. To acknowledge with Foucault that truth is not the "child of freedom" but of power/knowledge, that theory and practice cannot be separated in actuality but only cautiously and reservedly in reflection, is to always remain tentative in one's affirmations, suspicious even of one's feelings of certainty, recognizing that these feelings are only the concomitant of participating in a well-established episteme, or, as Rorty puts it, in normal discourse.

The courage to act and to think within an uncertain framework is not easily achieved. It may be that this is what is meant by faith. Faith is not a belief "in spite of," or a belief that I can act in a particular way without sufficient evidence. It is a stance of being, an acceptance of risk and openness, an affirmation of both the importance of human life (its dimension of ultimate significance) and the refusal to collapse that ultimacy into a static given, identifying it as definitively achieved in some concrete medium of its manifestation.

To engage in genealogy may itself be an act of faith, an expression of a willingness to live out conversion to the other as something that matters. To be critical of personal positions, to realize that they are partial, is also an act of faith, an acceptance of finitude and a refusal to cling to what may be transitory determinations of justice, freedom, and solidarity. Faith impels genealogy as it evokes conversion to the other. It also evokes critique as it challenges self-security. Faith does not bring certainty to liberation thought, though it may produce the motivating tension for critical thought and the ability to live within that tension.

The Critical Dialectic of Resistance

Granted that some tension with skepticism may be necessary for those of us who are oppressors and are aware of the power and tenacity of repressive apparatuses of power/knowledge, how does the tension between skepticism and commitment actually enable resistance to oppression? Does not resistance require some understanding of truth, even if it is only a prior definition of freedom? On what other basis does one resist than the awareness that something in human nature is being violated?

These questions are fair, but they imply a separation between theory and practice that is inadequate for critical theory. There is in resistance the operation of concepts of human nature, of some sort of theory. This theory is not the result of abstract speculation, however, but is grounded in concrete practice. To speak of liberation is to speak out of the experience of being oppressed, of resisting, and of being liberated. To speak of liberation is to make a particular type of statement, one not applicable to human being as such but to human being as it exists under conditions of oppression. It is the social and political equivalent of the traditional Christian language of sin and redemption. Those are not ontological categories but speak of modifications of human existence through the distortion of sin and release from that distortion. Resistance comes out of the experience of redemption, out of the practice of liberation from oppression, or from the experience of an alternate type of sociality that did not require structures of oppression. Knowledge that the criticized structures are not necessary emerges within the act of resistance.

Does the fact of resistance mean that the structure for which I (and others) work is an accurate reflection of human essence? To make such a statement is to claim too much. The weight of my critique lies not in its certain locus in an ontological structure but in its locus in a particular form of existence. My critique is not based on theoretical determinations of what should be the case but momentary experiences of what is the case.

My critique is grounded in actual insurrections, in the struggle between competing determinations of the nature of human sociality. I am able to work for freedom from sexism not because of a theoretical determination of the essence of human nature, an essence that is distorted by sexist structures, but because I have experienced a nonsexist type of existence. That actuality gives a theoretical analysis of patriarchy its plausibility. Recognizing the primacy of the historical leads to an acceptance of both the fragility and efficacy of this concrete, particular basis for resistance. To attempt to give these particular instances of liberation a "theoretical coronation" is both unnecessary and dangerously illusory (Foucault 1980b, 88).

Emphasis on the fragility and efficacy of a practical basis for resistance emerges from my experience in the women's movement. I am acutely aware of both the power of sisterhood, of concrete instances in which I and other women have been freed from sexism, and the tenuousness and rarity of that particular form of human sociality. It would be an act of the greatest folly for me to criticize sexism on the grounds of universally recognized values such as equality, the nature of moral persons, or any other determination of what characterizes the human, and thus women, as such.

I can only explain this reticence by turning to autobiography. I have always been a token. Although access to universalizing discourse, to participation in the work of philosophy and theology, is withheld from most women, I was encouraged to study those disciplines. The steady procession of my intellectual female friends turning to traditional pursuits seemed only to confirm the cultural stereotype of women as less rational and less aggressive than men. As a result, I defined myself as different from most members of my sex; I defined myself primarily in universal rather than gender-specific categories.

My blithe pursuit of universal structures (of course open to study by anyone with the requisite desire and ability) might have continued indefinitely. It was, however, interrupted by a rude reminder of the reality of the primacy of definition by gender. I confronted discrimination as a woman in my first job after college. This shattered any illusions I had about merit being a matter of pure achievement. I became aware that emphasis on universal human rights and the dignity of all persons obscured some people's sensitivity to the abrogation of those rights and that dignity on the basis of sex. I was faced with the paradox of seeing men who were fully committed to such universals as freedom and equality and yet were thoroughly sexist.

In light of this brief history, let me try to explain more clearly the irony I find in an oppressed person criticizing oppression in the name of universal values or ontological structures. The privilege to undergo the type of education that allows one to understand and use ontological categories and refer to universal values is a privilege denied many women in the present and most women in the past. It is a privilege denied those who are poor. Universal discourse is the discourse of the privileged. My inclusion in this community of discourse was not due to something intrinsic in the ideas and values themselves. These ideas did not immediately lead their proponents to advocate the full equality and humanity of all people, as is painfully evident in the struggle for the equal rights of black men and of women of all races in a society supposedly dedicated to the concept that "all men [*sic*] are created equal."

To use the very categories that masked my oppression in order to denounce it seems absurd. Better to refer to the particular events, the breakthroughs in practice that have challenged men's dominance: the emergence of the women's movement and its influence on women attempting to understand the forces that blocked them and the possibilities being opened to them. My critique of sexism is grounded in my experience of women who are excellent ministers in a denomination that did not ordain women, women who refuse definitions of themselves as sexual objects, women whose learning and political organizing broke patriarchal, individualistic, competitive models in the creation of communities that were cooperative and supportive.

To acknowledge and to accept this particular basis for resistance and critique is frightening. It is tempting to seek solace in the realm of universal values and in certain determinations of the nature of human being. But such refuge is an illusion. It is a denial that the ability to be aware of universal categories is accidental and fortuitous. Born twenty years ago or one hundred years ago (maybe even ten years in the future), such concerns might not be mine; they were not the concerns of most women in the past. I am aware of the oddity of my participation in the academy. Academic participation has not been the birthright of intellectual women. The inclusion of women in the worlds of academia, politics, and business may be a brief anomaly. Our gains could be as easily erased as were the gains of women in the Roman Empire, the gains of women in the first decades of the Christian movement, and the moves women made toward equality in England and the United States at the beginning of this century. Decisions that women participate in universal structures of human being will not protect or enable that participation. This change is a matter of changes in practices and in institutions, changes in not just knowledge but changes in apparatuses of power/knowledge. The primary challenge of liberation is not to construct the correct theory but the struggle to achieve freedom in history.

UNIVERSAL ACCOUNTABILITY
AND THE INTEGRITY OF THE PARTICULAR

Given such a locus in the particular, how can a liberation theologian claim that other systems of power/knowledge are oppressive? Can a feminist theology of liberation be anything other than provincial? If my definition of freedom is based on the experience of liberation from sexism, how can I address other forms of domination such as racism and capitalism? Concerns such as these seem to indicate the value of universally applicable definitions of freedom and justice.

Affirmations of the worth of all persons, concepts of universal human dignity, are not totally oppressive. They are liberating when they express a concern for the well-being of all people, when they lead us to care about justice for other groups of people, when they move us beyond a concern for our small social world. These ideas are not, however, liberating in their attempt to articulate that which is universal. Their liberating function lies in the concern they express for other people. This concern is, ironically, distorted by the very concepts that express it. To work for human rights, but to base our definition of those rights solely on the experience of one race, gender, or class, is itself oppressive.

The ambiguity intrinsic to a universal basis for resistance to injustice can be mitigated if the concern is expressed in terms of universal accountability rather than in terms of what is universally true about human being. Universal accountability may lead people to examine the impact of their social and economic system on the lives of other people. It is an expression of concern for other races and classes, for the lives of all those who are adversely affected by our political and economic systems. An affirmation of universal accountability means that we Americans must reevaluate our patterns of consumption; we are responsible to the rest of the world for our exploitation of scarce resources, for our use of them to support a lifestyle of relative affluence while millions die of starvation and millions live in the most abject poverty.

The idea of universal accountability leads quite naturally to another ideal, that of the integrity of the particular. While we may be accountable to all people for the economic and environmental costs of our way of life, the solution to the world's environmental problems, the solution to the problems of world hunger, is not necessarily the creation of a world government or the creation of standardized, uniform agricultural systems and systems of economic distribution. While we are responsible to each other, our responsibility may be met in innumerable ways. It is arrogant to assume that only the highly technological culture of the West can offer responsible, sustainable, equitable models of social organization.

What sort of social critique is possible for one guided by the two ideas of universal accountability and the integrity of the particular? I have found that protest against oppression is most effective and can best preclude a slide into oppressive discourse when it forswears the simple application of universal definitions of justice and freedom to other situations. A provisional definition of these terms—justice and freedom—is a component of resistance and critique. These preliminary definitions arise, however, not from speculation, but from practice, from an experience of freedom and justice in unique situations. Rootedness in the practical gives the definitions both their power and their limitations. They are inevitably limited by their formation in historically peculiar situations of oppression and liberation.

Given a particular experience of freedom and justice, how is it possible to criticize something like the torture of political prisoners in Chile? I should begin with my own experientially based definition of freedom and justice and then determine where the Chilean system contradicts those values. I should also look for resistance within the Chilean social system. Such resistance indicates that the system that seems oppressive has not completely established itself as definitive of humanity. If there is resistance, I should try to understand its basis—the experience of liberation or redemption that undergirds it—and seek to further its expression.

But what role is there for critique if there are no subjugated knowledges actively resisting a given system? If there is no resistance does that mean that the alternate ideals of freedom are provincial and not applicable? If oppression is so complete that there are no glimmers of resistance, I have to acknowledge that in this situation humanity as I know it has been obliterated. It is important to work against the extension of that form of humanity, but I must not deny its efficacy and power.

This may seem like giving up too soon. Is there not some power and purpose in denouncing oppression as invalid in essence albeit effective in practice? When a system of domination is weak, there may be some value in such a proclamation. Statements of condemnation may be valuable especially if there is a history of a connection between such statements and political action. Neither of these qualifications pertains in the United States. Militarism, for example, is so strong in the United States that political demonstrations against the nuclear arms race can be tolerated throughout the country and even inside the Pentagon.[3] Advanced capitalism, racism, and sexism are equally resilient. The ability of these systems of domination to withstand critique is enhanced by the failure of church bodies, political parties, and scholarly associations to translate rhetoric into action. In the United States we could conclude that the statement is the opiate of the people.

Universal denunciations of systems of oppression are a dangerous evasion of the relationship of power/knowledge, of the fragility of discourse. It is illusory to deny the reality of the defeat of a particular project of human being. To denounce the arms race, for example, as unjust is merely a declarative act. It does not actually challenge that structure and may even function as a dangerous illusion that in the denunciation something has been accomplished. Such statements may be evasions of the difficult strategic task, the determination of how people might create structures of justice. To challenge the truth of oppression is not to point to its intellectual or conceptual frailties, but to expose its frailties of practice, to disclose and nurture alternate forms of human community that challenge it on the level of daily operations of power/knowledge. To challenge oppression effectively is to point to its failure to determine the nature of human existence and to seek to extend the sphere of influence of alternate structures.

What are the advantages of such an apparently circumscribed form of resistance? It is both more effective and less tyrannical than other forms of resistance. Instead of assuming that universally valid goals can be ascertained from a particular situation, the present experience of liberation can mark the beginning of a definition of and struggle for further liberation. The temptation to define others' hopes for liberation must be avoided. The cultural genocide of an imperialistic Christianity is not accidental, but is grounded in such an arrogant approach to liberation. It is oppressive to "free" people if their own history and culture do not serve as the primary sources of the definition of their freedom.

In the struggle for liberation, the understanding of the nature of freedom that is held by the oppressors who wish to renounce their oppression of others must change. If such change does not occur, it is unlikely that the struggle for freedom is noncoercive. Instead, the error of Habermas is perpetuated: the assumption that an elite can effectively ascertain the contours of oppression and liberation and offer this theoretical work to the oppressed as a *fait accompli*.

The first advantage of the specific over the universal intellectual in resistance is that a thoroughly self-critical position avoids both the horrors of psychoanalysis, with its imposition of a binding "freedom" on women, and the tragedy of the suppression of dissent in some socialist systems. The oppressed must be heard by the oppressors as they name their own oppression and liberation. To deny those voices is to perpetuate oppression, even if it is done in the name of a universal concept of freedom.

Specific analyses emphasizing the strategic and the practical have a second advantage over more traditional theoretical critiques. The struggle against oppression gains power by drawing on people's heritage and experience, not merely on abstractions from their experience. A concept of freedom is most effective as it is rooted in the imagination of the people to be freed, if it does indeed speak to something in their experience and their history. The aim of a feminist theology of liberation is to seek the ground for resistance not on the level of the universal but on the level of the particular and the historical. This makes possible the recognition of unique or divergent forms of resistance and freedom.

Another advantage of the specific, strategic approach is its lack of naiveté, its recognition that oppressive definitions of humanity do have effects of truth—they have shaped human existence. This is a way of acknowledging what Doris Lessing refers to as the twist and damage wrought by the mass murders of the twentieth century. It is to acknowledge with Mary Daly the "patriarchal demons" that do influence how we think and know and act, that continue to emerge and imprison us when we least expect it (Daly 1978, 29–31). This approach reflects the awareness that liberation is not merely a matter of will and thought, but of practice and power, a matter of the transformation of systems of language and behavior that imprison us, a matter of the destruction of webs of oppression whose extent we only dimly ascertain.[4] To acknowledge this is to struggle at the level of the effects of truth of apparatuses of power/knowledge.

INTRINSIC RELATIVISM
OF A FEMINIST THEOLOGY OF LIBERATION

A feminist theology of liberation is intrinsically relative and thus maintains an ambiguous position. It has two contradictory strands: on the one hand, a relativist limitation of truth-claims and a qualified nihilism, an acceptance of the fact that might does shape reality, if not make right. On the other hand, nihilism and relativism are held in tension with a strong normative claim, an attempt to identify values and structures that can transform society and end oppression. Both strands are necessary. The tension between the two constitutes genuinely liberative theology and critical theory.

How can such a skeptical stance be reconciled with faith? Traditional understandings of faith imply just the opposite stance. There is no skepticism or nihilism in faith because those who are faithful are certain that nihilism is false, that there is a structure of meaning in which human existence participates. I concur that faith is opposed to a capitulation to nihilism, but I understand the contribution of genealogical work to be the clarification of the extent to which all truth is embedded in relations of power. It follows that we engage in a struggle with nihilism and not assume that its failure is in any sense guaranteed.

I realize that this skeptical attitude and the corresponding renunciation of universals is not found in the work of most liberation theologians. Yet I find such a renunciation required by my situation, which is that of a commitment to struggle against oppression by one who is an oppressor by reason of race and nationality. Without this skepticism and modesty, "liberation" can become another form of oppression: the imposition by an elite of a particular understanding of freedom.

There is another reason for skepticism, one also grounded in the historicity of discourse. When we address the modification of actual structures of human existence, it matters greatly if those modifications are not achieved. The discourse of liberation has no realm of consolation other than the historical. Hopes for redemption have failed in the past (as shown by the many holocausts of history) and may fail in the future. Nuclear holocaust and the destruction of the human species would mean the failure of Christianity and its promise of redemption. The economic and moral costs of the arms race themselves represent the failure of Christianity to establish conditions of justice.

As a Christian theologian, I feel compelled to take seriously the failure of Christianity. I evade this failure if I speak of the absolute truth of Christian faith as something that transcends its actualization in history. It is a perversion of a faith that claims to be concerned with the historical to locate its truth in an ahistorical realm, one unsullied by actual events in history.

It is important to note that this is not an "eschatological reservation." Skepticism is required, not because of the inevitable disparity between events in history and a transcendent ideal, but because of the fragility and unpredictability of the historical process itself: the possibility of the failure of a genuinely liberative ideal, or the oppressive impact of an ideal that is ostensibly liberating.

Skepticism about the truth of Christianity is not new. Ernst Bloch quotes a passage in which Marx and Engels claim that the failure of Christianity to transform history is evidence of its falsity:

> They would preach the kingdom of love in opposition to a rotten actuality and hatred . . . but when experience shows that this love has not been effective in 1800 years, has not changed social relationships and has not been able to build its kingdom, then it clearly follows that this love which has been unable to overcome hatred does not offer the dynamic power needed for social reforms. This love is consumed in sentimental assertions which cannot remove any actual conditions; it merely acts as a soporific on those whom it feeds with its sentimental mash [Marx and Engels 1971, 87].

This rhetoric is harsh, but the history to which it refers is as brutal as the critique. Christianity has failed. To acknowledge this failure and yet to remember and name the few instances of liberation that have occurred in communities of faith is to discover the relativism intrinsic to Christian faith.

My acknowledgment that the failures of Christian faith are as real as its successes has led me to a commitment to social change colored by skepticism and relativism. I have two overlapping reasons for my position. First, skepticism is required by the inescapable limitation and peril of discourse. Preventing the imposition of particular structures on other cultures, preventing the foreclosure of discourse or its limitation to an elite, requires a consciousness of the relativity of even a liberating Christianity's point of view, a suspicion as to the adequacy of its ability to determine the meaning of justice and freedom, and a willingness to have such ideas modified through dialogue and through evaluation in light of their effects of truth.

This skepticism leads me to a relativistic definition of humanity. I can claim with no hesitation that the actions of Hitler are manifestations of inhumanity, but I cannot be at all sure that my own understanding of humanity is not limited by the acceptance of some unseen form of oppression. Just as slavery and the treatment of women were for centuries not even recognized by sensitive theologians and people of faith as oppressive, it is possible that my thought and actions share in the perpetuation of as yet unrecognized forms of oppression. To be truly liberative, my feminist theology of liberation must not regard itself as the definitive exposition of the structure of freedom and justice, but must remain open to critiques like those of Foucault, critiques that reveal the dominations constitutive of even ostensibly humanizing procedures and reforms.

A second reason for relativism and skepticism is the need to remain consistently within one strand of the Jewish and Christian traditions, a strand that emphasizes that faith is not primarily declarative but revolutionary. The faith of the prophets and elements of the gospels proclaim an active process of redemption. These faiths motivate reform and action, not compliance with some already existing state of affairs. The direction of verification for this faith is practical. Knowledge that this faith is true comes only as it is effective, as it fulfills in action what it promises in hope: the blind see, the lame walk, the prisoners are loosed from their chains.

Outside of the actualization in history of these hopes for liberation, I do not know if they are ontologically or historically possible. There is always an element of risk in faith, an attempt to live on the basis of a wager that my hopes do indeed reflect an order of possibility. I can never know decisively that I am correct in my assessment. The history of Christian faith, its checkered past as both supporter of oppression and matrix of resistance, prevents a triumphal ecclesiology or christology, prevents an affirmation that sin has been conquered either in Jesus or through the church. There is more of the crucifixion than the resurrection in the history of the church.

I find it impossible to hold the universals of faith, the hope of universal solidarity, the hope for the total elimination of oppression, in any but a tensive and equivocal manner. My use of the universal concepts of freedom, justice, and solidarity is a tensive use for two reasons, one positive, one negative. The positive reason is that I simply cannot know the contours of a free society within an oppressive framework. I acknowledge the power of oppressive concepts of freedom and humanity, oppressive concepts both of the method of ascertaining "true statements" and of the continued internal operation of oppression in my attempts to define liberation and solidarity. Not only are my insights particular and finite, they are also tainted by sin, by the power of oppression. My struggle with oppression is ongoing and must not be forestalled by the hasty attempt to identify universal structures of human existence.

There is a second, more negative reason for the tensive application of universals: the application could be wrong, and this at any of three levels.

1. Efforts to create free, just communities could fail. Oppressive definitions of truth, of human nature, could win in practice, could have the overriding effect of truth. I cannot deny the victory of oppression in individual lives and social groups, in the type of human being created by sexism, the prison, the Gulag, the brutalities of war. In all these instances, what liberation theologians identify as oppressive is victorious. Lives have been irrevo-

cably shaped by oppressive structures. No amount of resistance can bring back the lives lost in the Nazi holocaust. What I regard as humane is defeated daily in the torture of the women and men of Latin America.

2. A second possible source of error in the application of universals is the too hasty imposition of commensuration, the refusal to listen to other descriptions of human existence, the assumption that I already have the definitive understanding in outline if not in full construction. To hold to truth as conversation rather than as reflection of essence is to live out an openness to continued change and modification, and is to relinquish the hope for an end to the conversation through the achievement of a complete understanding of liberation and justice. An awareness of the difficulty of the embodiment of structures of freedom and an openness to the likelihood of encountering alternate descriptions of solidarity and liberation require that I bring the definitions ascertained through my own experiences of liberation into dialogue with other interpretations, without assuming that the dialogue is to be one-sided, a "dialogue" of persuasion of the other.

3. Finally the most pressing reason for the maintenance of a tensive use of the ideals of freedom and solidarity is a tendency in liberation faith itself that impels me toward nihilism. This is the recognition of the possibility that my own experience of liberation within some particular forms of ecclesia is nothing but a fluke. That is, liberation and redemption do not reflect something that can be universalized, but reflect contingent configurations of human existence. The barbarism of the twentieth century—sexism, the threat of nuclear war, mass famine, the atrocities of Auschwitz, Vietnam, and El Salvador—may illustrate either the contingent or necessary limits of human morality.

Liberation Faith and Nihilism

The fear that liberation may be either structurally or contingently impossible is internally required by a liberating faith. Soelle and Metz speak of the dangerous memory of liberation faith as the refusal to forget the suffering of others in the past and in the present. Liberation faith is conversion to the other, the resistance to oppression, the attempt to live as though the lives of others matter. The paradox of this faith is that as resistance to oppression increases, as I begin to reflect on the dangerous memory of human suffering, it becomes more difficult to imagine a compensation for that suffering, even if similar suffering is eradicated in the future. The weight of past and present suffering is such that it seems irredeemable.

There is in liberation faith, with its conversion to the other, a sense of tragedy and loss. The loss of so many lives in history cannot be easily reconciled. To honestly live and believe as universal the imperative of love and freedom is to hope that suffering can be ended, to hope that all lives without liberation in history were not meaningless, but it is to work for this hope without the guarantee that such meaning is possible.

The human species may be fatally flawed. If there is anything universal about human nature, it may be our incapacity for community and justice. Christian faith and revolutionary struggles would then be only futile efforts to prevent the inevitable—the self-destruction of a tragically cruel and short-sighted form of life. Momentary actualizations of peace, justice, and freedom could be mere aberrations in the experience of a people incapable of survival. History, especially the record of the complicity of the Christian church with injustice, offers us little evidence to the contrary. I speak here as both an oppressor and a victim of oppression, well aware that patriarchy, militarism, and exploitation have characterized most of human history. Visions of equality, peace, and universal prosperity have, in the main, remained dreams and not realities.

This struggle with nihilism is not methodological, but is grounded in particular experiences within the peace movement and within Third World solidarity groups. The more I work to end the arms race, the less confidence I have that the dominant episteme can be vanquished. The more aware I become of the logic of war, of our dependence on a system of militarized sovereign states as a means of international order, and of the pervasiveness of patriarchy and its reliance on violence, the more fragile the contrasting episteme appears. I honestly do not know if the power of patriarchy and militarism can be broken before there is either a full-scale nuclear war or the unforgivable use of a single nuclear weapon.

To respond to the threat of nuclear war with protestations in the name of universal ideals such as the dignity of the human or the importance of freedom seems tragically absurd. To hold the values of the Enlightenment requires the condemnation of a society shaped by those values. The ideal of the rule of reason, of equality, and of justice has served as a screen for the irrationality of a technological society, the inequalities of a capitalistic world economy, and the injustice of a particular system of lawfulness threatening mass murder and global annihilation.

The twentieth century is the denouement of the Enlightenment and of Western ideals of civilization. We stand on the brink of extinction through nuclear holocaust or ecological disaster, a species whose greatest achievement in the last century has been the perfection of the art of genocide. From the first bombings of civilian targets by the Fascists in the Spanish Civil War, through Hitler's death camps and the genocidal warfare of the United States against the people of Vietnam, to the United States' flirtation with limited nuclear war, the "age of reason" has distinguished itself by its folly and cruelty. To speak of Christian ideals of love for the neighbor being in any sense true, or of the benefits of the rule of reason in an age gone mad in its acceptance and justification of oppression and exploitation, is an unspeakable outrage.

I find, therefore, in liberation faith an intrinsic correlation with doubt and a deepening awareness of the tragic dimensions of life. For as conversion to the other grows, as I experience more intensely the power of the dangerous memory of human suffering, doubt as to the possibility of reconciliation also rises. The elevation of the significance of particular human lives also makes it more difficult to imagine any way in which the dead can be redeemed or liberated. Even to speak of life after death is to use the language of hope and imagination, not the language of certainty, not the language of a realized or directly experienced form of reconciliation. If not directly ideological, a refusal of the weight and finality of history, this belief in an "afterlife" is at best an expression of hope that the dangerous memory of human suffering will somehow be reconciled.

The awareness of tragedy contains another ground for nihilism. At the heart of liberation faith, at the moments of actualization of its imperative of solidarity with the other, I have found a chasm that threatens to swallow both the possibility of hope and the realization of solidarity.

To explain this threat, I turn again to autobiography. I have done educational and political work against United States support of the government of El Salvador. My motive came from empathy with the poor of El Salvador and from an assessment of the cause of their suffering that placed responsibility for the torture and murder of thousands of people with the military and with an ineffective government unable either to control the military or to plan and implement adequate land reform.

My participation in a solidarity group was fairly straightforward and unproblematic until I saw a film about the revolution in El Salvador. Watching pictures of the police and the military drag people into the streets, beating and terrorizing them, hearing descriptions of tortured and mutilated bodies, feeling a fraction of the horror of that situation, shattered all my worlds of meaning. My ideals of universal solidarity faded in face of a suffering too great to name. My sanity was my insensitivity; my humanity was my inability not to care.

Can these two, the imperatives of sanity and of humanity, be reconciled? I do not know. I have not been able to reconcile them. I do not find many indications that our society embodies an adequate reconciliation. People are dying now, and our sane lack of caring is an intrinsic part of their deaths. Just as we have become inured to the human costs of our economic system, of our government's support of "friendly" authoritarian regimes, so we continue to blithely or callously or ignorantly benefit from those systems, failing to demand, in the name of the people, their radical transformation.

Awareness of human suffering, an awareness that impels me and others to work for revolution, carries with it the danger of madness and the frightening conclusion that even if we win now, even if injustice is eradicated, something irretrievable has been lost. Christian hope is a shallow and callous lie if it fails to be silenced or at least chastised by the voices of all those who suffer and die without relief.

I do not think that my sorrow is the result of inordinate guilt. I do not intend the focus of this description to be on myself as responsible for all evils. Nor is this guilt in another sense, an attempt to respond to an abstract imperative to love the other. I am speaking rather of a painful tension in liberation faith. Inasmuch as I have been freed by ecclesia, by sisterhood, so does my concern for others increase. My concern is not the fruit of obligation or guilt, but the gift of freedom and the superabundance of human love. My horror is due to the threat of insanity and despair that accompanies this life-giving gift.

Might we have here the theological equivalent of the mad philosopher? Foucault speaks suggestively of the madness of the philosopher,

> the experience of the philosopher who finds, not outside his [sic] language (the result of an external accident or imaginary exercise), but at the inner core of its possibilities, the transgressions of his [sic] philosophical being [Foucault 1977, 44].

I am speaking of the mad theologian, the liberation theologian who finds unspeakable and unbearable anguish to be the child of life-giving compassion and solidarity.

The recognition of the partial victory over oppression in the lives of the dead, the fear of its complete victory, and the struggle with nihilism motivates the paradoxical affirmation of a feminist theology of liberation. I am pulled back from self-indulgent ennui and despair only as I remain in community with those who are oppressed and are struggling against that oppression. To live in community with women helping other women and children recover from the trauma of rape, incest, and wife-abuse, with men working against rape by identifying and challenging the equation of sexuality and violence in male socialization, with women and men trying to create communities of nonviolence in a violent world reminds me that suffering is real, that it must be addressed even if one is not certain of its causes or aware of the best means of healing its damage. To remember the reality of oppression in the lives of people and to value those lives is to be saved from the luxury of hopelessness.

A Poetics of Revolution

The type of theology I have described affirms with Bloch "that learned hope is the signpost for this age—not just hope, but hope and the knowledge to take the way to it" (Bloch 1970, 91). Within this theological perspective, my struggle with nihilism and with alternate views of human destiny and capabilities is practical. This theology emerges from the struggle to create, not merely to proclaim, a human community that embodies freedom. The verification of this struggle is not conceptual, but practical: the successful process of enlightenment and emancipation, a process that is open and self-critical. This theology emerges from an effort to live on the edge, accepting both the power and the peril of discourse, engaging in a battle for truth with a conscious preference for the oppressed.

A feminist theology of liberation understands Christianity as a perspective that is not already true but that becomes true where human beings are freed. Feminist theology is located in the horizon of the memory of the many times and places where Christian faith and hopes are not actualized and the Christian definition of the nature of human being is defaced or obliterated. Given this horizon, the search for the verification of Christian faith is a practical one. The primary evidence of the truth of Christianity is its successful actualization. The primary threat to it, the basic denial of its truth, is the actualization of structures that subvert solidarity, that destroy human dignity, that take human lives.

The truth of faith is not found in theoretical certainty about the eventual necessary victory within history of the Christian project. The truth of faith is found rather in struggle or in a certain way of determining the true, a way that enhances and creates solidarity and full participation in the making of culture and society. Within a feminist theology of liberation, faith is not the denial of risk, but living within the fragile balance of absolute commitment and infinite suspicion.

To live for a particular definition of human being without a guarantee of its historical possibility is not an easy task. The particular ideal of a feminist theology of liberation compounds the risk. The ideal of solidarity is dangerous. Solidarity may be impossible: full empathy with the suffering of all people would surely lead to insanity, to the collapse of all conventional structures of meaning. I do not even know what the results would be if a person or community acknowledged with total seriousness the suffering of those people within their immediate field of vision.

My skepticism is caused not only by an awareness of the difficulties of social and political transformation and of the possibility of failure; it is also rooted in the extreme contingency and probable arbitrariness of my own projects. My concept of solidarity has unknown determinants; its ramifications are unpredictable; it is tenuous and fragile. And yet, my commitment to solidarity leads to as active a struggle for its implementation as if I were certain of its future success and inherent possibility.

A feminist theology of liberation operates within a paradoxical tension, making transcultural claims and normative judgments, yet always remaining open to challenge and modification, trying to avoid any sort of moral imperialism or triumphalism. The value of Christian faith may be that it gives us the ability to live with that tension. If the life of faith is one of absolute commitment and infinite suspicion, the ground of commitment is neither rationalistic nor authoritarian. It is possible to avoid both the intellectual certainty of rational explanation and the mysterious certainty of an authoritative revelation and faith.

A feminist theology of liberation can perhaps best be understood as a poetics of revolution. Just as poetry can sacrifice meaning to explanation, so theology in its search for the clarity and precision of absolutes is certain to lose the meaning of revolution: the rich profusion of possibilities, the vision of new worlds to be attained. In its critique and in its vision, a feminist theology of liberation should remain concrete and open to further analyses and refinements. It is a discourse that is imbued with the particular tragedy of human existence—the dangerous memory of despair, barrenness, suffering —and with the particular moments of liberation—the equally dangerous memory of historical actualizations of freedom and community.

Notes

CHAPTER 1

1. The problem of liberal theology is examined in the following works: Gordon Kaufman, *An Essay on Theological Method* (1979); Edward Farley, *Ecclesial Man: A Social Phenomenology of Faith and Reality* (1975); Langdon Gilkey, *Naming the Whirlwind: The Renewal of God-Language* (1969); and David Tracy, *Blessed Rage for Order: The New Pluralism in Theology* (1975). The fact that this is a problem for *liberal* theology and not true of all theologies is demonstrated in Harvey Cox's analysis of the vitality of both fundamentalist theology and liberation theology: *Religion in the Secular City: Toward a Postmodern Theology* (1984).

2. "Memory has a fundamental theological importance as what may be termed anamnetic solidarity or solidarity in memory with the dead and the conquered which breaks the grip of history as a history of triumph and conquest interpreted dialectically or as evolution. . . . Memory can have a very decisive ecclesiological importance in defining the Church as the public vehicle transmitting a dangerous memory in the systems of social life" (Metz 1980, 184).

3. John B. Cobb, Jr., *Process Theology as Political Theology* (1984).

4. Edward Farley defines ecclesia as "an intersubjectively shaped redemptive consciousness" (Farley 1975, xiv). Although it is collective or communal, ecclesia is not synonymous with the church as an institution.

CHAPTER 2

1. Conversation with Lark D'Helen, fall 1982.

2. "It is clear that there is such an underground Bible, both *infra* and *contra* and *ultra* the heteronomous light of the theocratic firmament. . . . There, then, . . . is the true *visio haeretica*, with (often suppressed) violent kicking against oppression, inspired by an unparalleled *expectation* of the real Utterly-other with which the world will one day be filled" (Bloch 1972, 82).

3. Segundo 1976, 110. See also chapter 4.

4. This phenomenon is given a fuller examination in Mary Daly, *Pure Lust: Elemental Feminist Philosophy* (1984).

CHAPTER 3

1. I am referring to the phenomenon described by Edward Farley as either the house of authority or the way of authority. He defines this phenomenon as follows: "It [the way of authority] is little more than a code word for certain features of classical Catholic and Protestant ways of grounding claims, namely in some specifia-

ble entity (Scripture, text, church father) whose truth character has an a priori quality. As an authority, the text could be a norm for truth but could not itself be subject to something outside itself to determine its truth" (Farley 1983, 26).

2. Conversation with Sharon Parks, spring 1983.

3. This is the term used by Foucault to describe the resistance of excluded discourses (Foucault 1980b, 81).

CHAPTER 4

1. Chief Seattle in 1855, quoted by Jeanne Rollins, "Liberation and the Native American," in *Theology in the Americas*, edited by Sergio Torres and John Eagleson (Maryknoll, N.Y.: Orbis Books, 1976), p. 203.

CHAPTER 5

1. The phrase quoted in the title of this chapter is from Stevens's "The Sail of Ulysses," in *The Palm at the End of the Mind*, edited by Holly Stevens (New York: Random House, Vintage Press, 1972), p. 392.

2. "Inescapable romance, inescapable choice / Of dreams, disillusion as the last illusion, / Reality as a thing seen by the mind" (Wallace Stevens, "An Ordinary Evening in New Haven," in *The Palm at the End of the Mind*, p. 333).

3. This was borne out at a series of demonstrations sponsored by Jonah House held at and within the Pentagon in 1980.

4. The metaphor "webs of oppression" was developed in an unpublished paper by Joel Martin (spring 1983).

Works Cited

Bloch, Ernst. 1970. *Man On His Own: Essays in the Philosophy of Religion*. New York: Herder & Herder.

———. 1972. *Atheism in Christianity: The Religion of the Exodus and the Kingdom*. New York: Herder & Herder.

Brown, Robert McAfee. 1976. "A Preface and a Conclusion." In *Theology in the Americas*. Ed. Sergio Torres and John Eagleson. Maryknoll, N.Y.: Orbis Books.

Cobb, John B., Jr. 1984. *Process Theology as Political Theology*. Philadelphia: Westminster Press.

Coleridge, Samuel Taylor. 1883. *Aids to Reflection*. London and New York: G. Bell.

Collins, Sheila. 1974. *A Different Heaven and Earth*. Valley Forge, Pa.: Judson Press.

Cone, James. 1969. *Black Theology and Black Power*. New York: Seabury Press.

———. 1975. *God of the Oppressed*. New York: Seabury Press.

Cox, Harvey. 1984. *Religion in the Secular City: Toward a Postmodern Theology*. New York: Simon and Schuster.

Daly, Mary. 1973. *Beyond God the Father: Toward a Philosophy of Women's Liberation*. Boston: Beacon Press.

———. 1978. *Gyn/Ecology: The Metaethics of Radical Feminism*. Boston: Beacon Press.

———. 1984. *Pure Lust: Elemental Feminist Philosophy*. Boston: Beacon Press.

Farley, Edward. 1975. *Ecclesial Man: A Social Phenomenology of Faith and Reality*. Philadelphia: Fortress Press.

———. 1983. *Theologia: The Fragmentation and Unity of Theological Education*. Philadelphia: Fortress Press.

Foucault, Michel. 1972. *The Archaeology of Knowledge and the Discourse on Language*. New York: Harper & Row.

———. 1973. *The Order of Things: An Archaeology of the Human Sciences*. New York: Vintage Books.

———. 1975. *The Birth of the Clinic: An Archaeology of Medical Perception*. New York: Vintage Books.

———. 1976. *The Archaeology of Knowledge*. New York: Harper & Row

———. 1977. *Language, Counter-Memory, Practice: Selected Essays and Interviews*. Ed. Donald F. Bouchard. Ithaca, N.Y.: Cornell University Press.

———. 1979. *Discipline and Punish: The Birth of the Prison*. New York: Vintage Books.

———. 1980a. *History of Sexuality*. New York: Vintage Books.

———. 1980b. *Power/Knowledge: Selected Interviews and Other Writings, 1972–1977*. New York: Pantheon Books.

Foucault, Michel, and Gilles Deleuze. 1977. "Intellectuals and Power." In Foucault 1977.

Gilkey, Langdon. 1969. *Naming the Whirlwind: The Renewal of God-Language.* Indianapolis and New York: Bobbs-Merrill.

Gordon, Colin. 1980. "Afterword." In Foucault 1980b.

Gutiérrez, Gustavo. 1973. *A Theology of Liberation: History, Politics and Salvation.* Maryknoll, N.Y.: Orbis Books.

———. 1978. "Two Theological Perspectives." In *The Emergent Gospel.* Ed. Sergio Torres and Virginia Fabella. Maryknoll, N.Y.: Orbis Books.

Habermas, Jurgen. 1973. *Legitimation Crisis.* Boston: Beacon Press.

Hacking, Ian. 1981. In *New York Review of Books*, 28:8, May 14.

Harrington, D. 1971. "Ernst Käsemann on the Church in the New Testament." In *Heythrop Journal*, XII.

Jay, Martin. 1973. *The Dialectical Imagination: A History of the Frankfurt School and the Institute of Social Research, 1923–1950.* Boston: Little, Brown.

Johnson, Paul. 1979. *A History of Christianity.* New York: Atheneum.

Käsemann, Ernst. 1964. "The Canon of the New Testament and the Unity of the Church." In *Essays on New Testament Themes.* London: SCM Press.

———. 1971. "Justification and Salvation History in the Epistle to the Romans." In *Perspectives on Paul.* Philadelphia: Fortress Press.

Kaufman, Gordon. 1979. *An Essay on Theological Method.* AAR Studies in Religion, no. 11. Rev. ed. Missoula, Mont.: Scholars Press.

———. 1983. "Nuclear Eschatology and the Study of Religion." In *Journal of the American Academy of Religion*, LI/1 (March 1983).

Lernoux, Penny. 1982. *Cry of the People: The Struggle for Human Rights in Latin America, The Catholic Church in Conflict with U.S. Policy.* New York: Penguin Books.

Lessing, Doris. 1964. "Landlocked." In *Children of Violence.* New York: Simon and Schuster.

Luther, Martin. 1959. *Luther the Expositor: Luther's Works Companion.* Ed. Jaroslav Pelikan. St. Louis: Concordia.

McFague, Sallie. 1975. *Speaking in Parables: A Study in Metaphor and Theology.* Philadelphia: Fortress Press.

———. 1982. *Metaphorical Theology: Models of God in Religious Language.* Philadelphia: Fortress Press.

Marx, Karl. 1964. "Contributions to the Critique of Hegel's Philosophy of Right." In *Marx and Engels on Religion.* New York: Schocken Books.

Marx, Karl, and Frederick Engels. 1971. "Circular Letter Against Kriege, May 11, 1846." In Ernst Bloch, *On Karl Marx.* New York: Herder & Herder.

Metz, Johann Baptist. 1980. *Faith in History and Society: Toward a Practical Fundamental Theology.* New York: Seabury Press.

Míguez Bonino, José. 1974. *Doing Theology in a Revolutionary Situation.* Philadelphia: Fortress Press.

———. 1976. *Christians and Marxists: The Mutual Challenge to Revolution.* Grand Rapids, Mich.: Eerdmans. ✷

Miranda, José. 1974. *Marx and the Bible: A Critique of the Philosophy of Oppression.* Maryknoll, N.Y.: Orbis Books.

———. 1977. *Being and the Messiah: The Message of St. John.* Maryknoll, N.Y.: Orbis Books.

Plaskow, Judith. 1980. *Sex, Sin and Grace: Women's Experience and the Theologies of Reinhold Niebuhr and Paul Tillich.* Washington, D.C.: University Press of America.

Rich, Adrienne. 1978a. "Natural Resources." In *The Dream of a Common Language*. New York: W.W. Norton.

———. 1978b. "Transcendental Etude." In *The Dream of a Common Language*. New York: W.W. Norton.

Ricoeur, Paul. 1974. "Religion, Atheism, and Faith." In *The Conflict of Interpretations: Essays in Hermeneutics*. Evanston, Ill.: Northwestern University Press.

———. 1975. *Semeia 4: Paul Ricoeur on Biblical Hermeneutics*. Ed. John Dominic Crossan. Missoula, Mont.: Scholars Press.

Rollins, Jeanne. 1976. "Liberation and the Native American." In *Theology in the Americas*. Ed. Sergio Torres and John Eagleson. Maryknoll, N.Y.: Orbis Books.

Rorty, Richard. 1979. *Philosophy and the Mirror of Nature*. Princeton, N.J.: Princeton University Press.

———. 1981. In *London Review of Books*. 19 Feb.–4 March.

Ruether, Rosemary Radford. 1975. *New Woman/New Earth: Sexist Ideologies and Human Liberation*. New York: Seabury Press.

———. 1981. " 'Basic Communities': Renewal at the Roots." In *Christianity and Crisis*, 41:14 (Sept. 21).

Saiving, Valerie. 1979. "The Human Situation: A Feminine View." In *Womanspirit Rising: A Feminist Reader in Religion*. Ed. Carol P. Christ and Judith Plaskow. San Francisco: Harper & Row.

Schleiermacher, Friedrich. 1928. *The Christian Faith*. Edinburgh: T. & T. Clark.

Segundo, Juan Luis. 1976. *The Liberation of Theology*. Maryknoll, N.Y.: Orbis Books.

Shelley, John. 1974. "Introduction." In Soelle 1974.

Sheridan, Alan. 1980. *Michel Foucault: The Will to Truth*. New York: Tavistock.

Sobrino, Jon. 1978. *Christology at the Crossroads: A Latin American Approach*. Maryknoll, N.Y.: Orbis Books.

———. 1980. Unpublished paper delivered at Theology in the Americas Conference, Detroit, Michigan.

Soelle, Dorothee. 1974. *Political Theology*. Philadelphia: Fortress Press.

———. 1978. *Beyond Mere Dialogue: On Being Christian and Socialist*. The 1977 Earl Lectures at the Pacific School of Religion. Detroit, Mich.: American Christians Toward Socialism.

———. 1983. *The Arms Race Kills Even without War*. Philadelphia: Fortress Press.

Steiner, George. 1971. In *Bluebeard's Castle: Some Notes Toward the Redefinition of Culture*. New Haven, Conn.: Yale University Press.

Stevens, Wallace. 1972. *The Palm at the End of the Mind: Selected Poems and a Play*. Ed. Holly Stevens. New York: Random House, Vintage Press.

Tillich, Paul. 1950. *The Shaking of the Foundations*. New York: C. Scribner & Sons.

———. 1957. *Dynamics of Faith*. New York: Harper & Row.

———. 1973. *Systematic Theology*. Vol. 1. Chicago: University of Chicago Press.

Tracy, David. 1975. *Blessed Rage for Order: The New Pluralism in Theology*. New York: Seabury Press.

Welch, Claude. 1972. *Protestant Thought in the Nineteenth Century 1799–1870*. Vol. I. New Haven: Yale University Press.

Zahrnt, Heinz. 1966. *The Question of God: Protestant Theology in the Twentieth Century*. New York: Harcourt Brace Jovanovich.

INDEX

Compiled by James Sullivan